D0722354

Library
Western Wyoming Community College

Merry Christmas to all!

From Thomas Nast's "Christmas Drawings for the Human Race."
Copyright 1889 by Harper and Brothers.

394.268
W168s
1970

THE STORY OF SANTA KLAUS

TOLD FOR CHILDREN OF ALL
AGES FROM SIX TO SIXTY

BY

WILLIAM S. WALSH

AND ILLUSTRATED BY ARTISTS OF ALL AGES
FROM FRA ANGELICO TO HENRY HUTT

DETROIT
Gale Research Company • Book Tower
1970

This is a facsimile reprint of the 1909
edition published by Moffat, Yard and
Company, New York.

Library of Congress Catalog Card Number: 68-58166
ISBN 0-8103-3370-8

CONTENTS

LIST OF ILLUSTRATIONS

THE STORY OF SANTA KLAUS

THE STORY OF SANTA KLAUS

CHAPTER I

WHO IS SANTA KLAUS?

IF you go to England you will find many people there who have never heard of Santa Klaus. Only the other day a leading London paper confessed that it could not understand why a magazine for children should be called St. Nicholas.

Now if you were asked the question which heads this chapter do you think you could answer it so as to make an Englishman understand who Santa Klaus is? Could you also explain what connection Saint Nicholas has with children?

Of course you might glibly reply:

"Santa Klaus is the Dutch diminutive (or pet name) for Saint Nicholas, and Saint Nicholas is the patron saint of boys and girls."

But the Englishman might want to know more than this. Perhaps you yourself would be glad to know more. It is for the purpose of supplying you with information that I have prepared this little book.

Let us begin with the legends which concern this holy man and see what help they will give us. I say let us begin with the legends, because history itself tells us little or nothing about the saint beyond the fact that he was Bishop of a town called Myra in Asia Minor and that he died about the year 342. Legend fills out these meagre details with many a pretty story which throws a kindly light upon the character of good Saint Nicholas.

You know what a legend is? It means a story which was not put into writing by historians at the time when the thing is said to have happened, but which has been handed down from father to son for hundreds and sometimes for thousands of years. It may or may not have had some basis of truth at the beginning. But after passing from mouth to mouth in this fashion it is very likely to lose what truth it once possessed. Still, even if the facts are not given in just the manner in which they happened there is nearly always some useful moral wrapped up in the fiction that has grown around the facts. That is why wise and learned men are glad to collect these legends from the lips of the peasants and other simple minded folk who have learned them at their mothers' knee, and who believe that they are all true. These legends are called by the general name of folk-lore.

St. Nicholas as the patron of children.
Italian print.

Two brothers of the name of Grimm once collected into a book the folk-lore of their native country, Germany.   This book is known to you as Grimm's Fairy Tales.   Hans Christian Andersen also found among the legends of Denmark some of the prettiest and most fanciful of his tales.

Now stories concerning Saint Nicholas abound in almost every country of Europe, for almost every country except Great Britain is interested in his name and fame.   He may, indeed, be called the busiest of all the saints.   In the first place legend makes him the patron saint of children all over the world, no matter of what sex or color or station in life.   Ever childlike and humble, so we are told by a quaint old author, "he keepeth the name of a child, for he chose to keep the virtues of meekness and simpleness.   Thus he lived all his life in virtues with this child's name, and therefore children do him worship before all other saints."

One might think that to be a patron of the world's children would keep one saint pretty busy, even if it did not exhaust his energies.   Not so with Saint Nicholas.   He occupies his spare moments as the protector of the weak against the strong, of the poor against the rich, of the servant and the slave against the master.   Because he once calmed a storm he is the patron of travellers and sailors and of many seaport towns.   Because he once converted a gang of robbers and made them restore their booty to the men they had robbed he is still thought to retain a kindly interest in thieves.

Moreover he is the patron of the largest of all European countries, the empire of Russia.

Now we will make our promised examination of the legends which have gathered around this saint and given him a fame so widespread.

Saint Nicholas is said to have been born in a town called Potara in Asia Minor. To the great wonder of his nurses he stood up in a tub on the day of his birth with his hands clasped together and his eyes raised to heaven and gave thanks to God for having brought him into the world. It is added that on Wednesday and Fridays, (both fast days in the early Church) he would refuse to take milk until the going down of the sun.

His parents died when he was very young. As they were wealthy they left him well provided with the world's goods. But he would not accept them for himself. Instead he used them for the good of the poor and of the Church.

When he was old enough he studied for the priesthood in the town of Myra and was ordained as soon as he had reached man's estate. He at once set sail on a voyage to the Holy Land to visit the tomb of Jesus Christ in Jerusalem. On the way a dreadful storm arose. The winds howled and whistled, the great waves shook the vessel from stem to stern.

The captain and the sailors who had been used to

The consecration of St. Nicholas.
Old print

bad weather pretty much all their lives declared that this was the worst storm they had ever known. Indeed they had given up all hope when the young Nicholas bade them be of good cheer.

His prayers soon calmed the wind and the waves, so that the ship reached Alexandria safe and sound. There the saint landed and made the greater part of the journey from Alexandria to Jerusalem on foot.

Returning by sea, he wished to go straight back to Myra. The captain, however, would not obey his orders and tried to make the port of Alexandria. Then Saint Nicholas prayed again and another great storm arose. And the captain was so frightened by this evidence of the saint's powers that he gladly listened to his request and headed the ship towards Myra.

In the year 325 Nicholas, then still a young man, was elected Bishop of Myra. On the day of his consecration to that office a woman brought into the church a child which had fallen into the fire and been badly burned. Nicholas made the sign of the cross over the child and straightway restored it to health. That is the first of his miracles which showed the interest that he took in children.

Two other miracles which are still more famous are thought to foreshadow the fame he has won since his death as the patron of children and the bearer of gifts to them at the holy Christmas season.

Among the members of his flock (so runs the first story) there was a certain nobleman who had three young daughters. From being rich he became poor,—so poor that he could not afford to support his daughters nor supply the dowry which would enable him to marry them off. For in those days, as even now in many countries in Europe, young men expected that a bride should bring with her a sum of money from her parents with which the young couple could start housekeeping. This is called the dowry.

Over and over the thought came into the nobleman's mind to tell his daughters that they must go away from home and seek their own living as servants or in even meaner ways. Shame and sorrow alone held him dumb. Meanwhile the maidens wept continually, not knowing what to do, and having no bread to eat. So their father grew more and more desperate.

At last the matter came to the ears of Saint Nicholas. That kindly soul thought it a shame that such things should happen in a Christian country. So one night when the maidens were asleep and their father sat alone, watching and weeping, Saint Nicholas took a handful of gold and tying it up in a handkerchief, or as some say placing it in a purse, set out for the nobleman's house.

He considered how he might best bestow the money without making himself known. While he stood hes-

St. Nicholas and the three maidens.

Fifteenth century painting.

itating the moon came up from behind a cloud, and
showed him an open window. He threw the purse
containing the gold in through the window and it fell
at the feet of the father.

Greatly rejoiced was the old gentleman when the
money plumped down beside him. Picking up the
purse he gave thanks to God and presented it to his
eldest daughter as her dowry. Thus she was enabled
to marry the young man whom she loved.

Not long afterwards Saint Nicholas collected together another purse of money and threw it into the
nobleman's house just as he had done before. Thus
a dowry was provided for the second daughter.

And now the curiosity of the nobleman was excited.
He greatly desired to know who it was that had come
so generously to his aid. So he determined to watch.
When the good saint came for a third time and made
ready to throw in the third purse, he was discovered,
for the nobleman seized him by the skirt of his robe
and flung himself at his feet, crying:

"Oh, Nicholas, servant of God, why seek to hide
thyself?"

And he kissed the holy man's feet and hands. But
Saint Nicholas made him promise that he would tell
no one what had occurred.

The second legend is much more wonderful. It
tells how Saint Nicholas was once travelling through
his diocese at a time when the people had been driven

to the verge of starvation. One night he put up at an inn kept by a very cruel and very wicked man, though nobody in the neighborhood yet suspected his guilt.

This monster, finding that the famine had made beef and mutton extremely scarce and greatly raised their price, had conceived the idea of filling his pantry with the fat juicy corpses of children whom he kidnapped, killed and served up to his guests in all varieties of nicely cooked dishes and under all sorts of fancy names.

Nobody could guess how he alone of all the innkeepers in that neighborhood could maintain a table so well supplied with meats, boiled and roasted, and stews and hashes and nice tasty soups.

But no sooner had a dish of this human flesh been served up to the saint than he discovered the horrible truth.

Leaping to his feet he poured out his anger in bitter but righteous words. Vainly the landlord fawned and cringed and protested that he was innocent. Saint Nicholas simply walked over to the tub where the bodies of the children had been salted down. All he had to do was to make the sign of the cross over the tub, and lo! three little boys, who had been missing for days, arose alive and well, and, coming out of the tub, knelt at the feet of the saint.

St. Nicholas resuscitating the schoolboys.

Old Neapolitan print.

All the other guests of the inn were struck dumb
the miracle. The children were restored to their
mother, who was a widow. As to the landlord, he
was taken out and stoned to death, as he richly de-
served to be.

Another of St. Nicholas' miracles shows that he
had a kind heart for grown-ups as well, as for the
young folk. A revolt having broken out in Phrygia,
Emperor Constantine sent a number of his tribunes
to quell it. When they had reached Myra, the bishop
invited them to his table so that they would not quar-
ter themselves on poorer citizens, who might be ill
able to afford their keep.

A grand banquet was served up to them. As host
and guests were preparing to sit down, news was
brought into the hall that the prefect of the city had
condemned three men to death, on a false accusation
that they were rebels. They had just been led to
execution and the whole city was in a ferment of excitement over this terrible act of injustice.

Nicholas rose at once from the table. Followed
by his guests he ran to the place of execution. There
he found the three men kneeling on the ground, their
eyes bound with bandages, and the executioner standing over them waving his bared sword in the air.
Nicholas snatched the sword out of his hand. Then
he ordered the men to be unbound. No one dared

to disobey him.   Even the prefect fell upon his knees and humbly craved forgiveness, which was granted with some reluctance.

Meanwhile the tribunes, looking on at the scene, were filled with wonder and admiration.   They, too, cast themselves at the feet of the holy man and besought his blessing.   Then, having feasted their fill on the banquet that had been provided for them, the tribunes continued their journey to Phrygia.

They, too, it was decreed were to fall under the ban of a false accusation.   During their absence from Constantinople, Constantine's mind had been poisoned against them by their enemies.   Immediately on their return he cast them into prison.   They were tried and condemned to death as traitors.   From the dungeon into which they had been cast to await the carrying out of this sentence they sent out a piteous prayer to St. Nicholas for assistance.   Though he was hundreds of miles away, he heard them.

And that same night he appeared to Constantine in a dream, commanding him to release these men and to declare them innocent,—threatening him at the same time with the wrath of God if he refused.   Constantine did not refuse.   He took the saint's word for their innocence, pardoned them, and set them free. Next morning he despatched them to Myra to thank Saint Nicholas in person for their happy deliverance. As a thank offering they bore him a copy of the

Bishop Nicholas.
From old Italian print.

gospels, written in letters of gold, and bound in a cover embossed with pearls and precious stones.

Nor did the saint's miracles end with his life. Even after death he listened from his high place in heaven to the prayers of the humblest and gladly hastened to their assistance when they asked for help in the right spirit and at the right time.

Here are three legends which have been especially popular in literature and art.

A Jew of Calabria, hearing of the wonderful miracles which had been performed by Saint Nicholas, stole his image out of the parish church and bore it away to his home. There he placed it in his parlor. And when, next day, he had made ready to go out for the morning he commended all his treasures to the care of the saint, impudently threatening that his image would be soundly thrashed if he failed in his trust. No sooner was the Jew's back turned, however, than robbers broke into the house and carried off all its treasures. Great was the Jew's wrath when he returned. Bitter were the reproaches he hurled at the saint. Many and fierce were the whacks he bestowed upon the image.

That very night Saint Nicholas, all bruised and bleeding, appeared to the robbers, and commanded them immediately to restore what they had taken. Terrified at the vision they leaped to their feet, collected the plunder, and brought it back to the Jew's house.   The Jew was so astonished at the miracle that he was easily converted to Christianity and baptized.

There was a wealthy man who, though married, had no son to inherit his estate.   This man vowed that if Saint Nicholas would provide him with an heir he would present a cup of gold to the saint's altar at Myra.   Saint Nicholas heard the prayer and, through his intercession, God sent the childless man a son.   At once the father ordered the cup of gold to be prepared.   When it was finished, however, it seemed so beautiful in his eyes that he decided to keep it for himself and offer the saint a meaner one made of silver.   When this, too, was finished, the merchant with his son set out to make the presentation. On the journey he stopped by a river to quench his thirst.   Taking out the golden cup he bade the son fetch him some water.   In obeying the child fell into the river and was drowned.

Weeping bitter tears of repentance the merchant appeared in the church of Saint Nicholas and there made his offering of the silver cup.   But the cup would not stay where it was put.   Once, twice, thrice, it fell off the altar.

While all the people stared with astonishment, behold the drowned boy appeared before them,—standing on the steps of the altar with the golden cup in his hand.   Full of joy and gratitude, the father of-

St. Nicholas of Bari.
Old Italian print.

fered both the cups to the saint and bore his son home
with thanksgivings to God and to His saint.

A certain rich merchant, himself a Christian, dwelt
on the borders of a heathen country. He cultivated
a special devotion to Saint Nicholas. One day his
only son was taken captive by some of the wicked
neighbors across the boundary line and sold into
slavery. The lad finally became the property of the
pagan king, and served him as his cup-bearer.

One day, while filling the royal cup at dinner he
suddenly remembered that it was December 6, and
the feast of Saint Nicholas. He burst into tears at
the thought that his family were even then gathered
around the dinner table in honor of their patron.

"Why weepest thou?" testily asked the king.
"Seest thou not that thy tears fall into my cup and
spoil my wine?"

And the boy answered through his sobs:

"This is the day when my parents and my kindred
are met together in great joy to honor our good Saint
Nicholas; and I, alas! am far away from them."

Then the pagan blasphemer swore a good round
oath and said:

"Great as is thy Saint Nicholas, he cannot save thee
from my hand!"

Hardly were the words out of his mouth when a
whirlwind shook the palace. A flash of lightning

was followed by a loud peal of thunder and lo! Saint Nicholas himself stood in the midst of the affrighted feasters. He caught the youth up by the hair of his head so suddenly that he had no time to drop the royal cup, and whirled him through the air at a prodigious speed until, a few moments later, he landed him in his home. The family were gathered in the dining room when saint and boy made their appearance,—the father being even then engaged in distributing the banquet to the poor, beseeching in return that they would offer up their prayers in behalf of his captive son.

CHAPTER II

St. Nicholas, as I have said, died in the year 342 and was buried with great honor in the cathedral at Myra.

Being the patron saint of such roving folk as sailors, merchants and travellers it was only natural that his body should have lain in perpetual peril from thievish hands. The relics of saints were highly prized because it was held that they performed miracles on behalf of the townsfolk and of the strangers who visited their shrines. Of course the relics of so great and popular a saint as Nicholas were especially coveted, and most so by the classes of whom he was the patron.

In those rude days it was believed that no saint was greatly troubled by the manner in which his body was procured. Even if it were stolen and reburied elsewhere by the robbers themselves the body worked miracles in its new abode as cheerfully as it had done in the old one. Moreover it drew trade and custom to any city in which it was enshrined and so brought wealth to the people of the entire neighborhood.

In fact pilgrims from various parts of the world came in crowds to the shrine at Myra. As the fame of Saint Nicholas increased so did the value of his relics. At various times during the first six centuries after his burial attempts were made to carry off his body by force or by fraud.

None of these attempts was successful until, in the year 1084, certain merchants from the city of Bari, in southeastern Italy, landed at Myra to find that the entire countryside had been laid waste by an invasion of the Turks. All the men who could bear arms had gathered together and were now gone in pursuit of the invaders. Three monks only had been left behind to stand guard over the shrine of Saint Nicholas.

It was an easy task for the merchants of Bari to overpower these monks, break open the coffin which contained the body and bear it away with them to their own city.

Here it was received with great joy. A fine new church was built on the site of an old one which had been dedicated to Saint Stephen and which was now torn down to make room for its successor. This was to serve as a shrine for the stolen body. The new church is still standing and though it is now old it is still magnificent. In a crypt or vault under its high altar lies all that was mortal of the one-time Bishop of Myra. On the very day of the re-burial, so it is said, no less than thirty people who attended

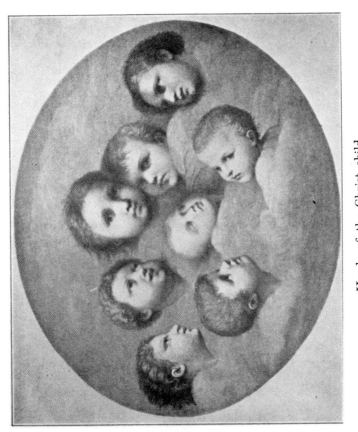

Heads of the Christ child.

Selected from Raphael's pictures.

the ceremony were cured of their various ailments.

Such is the story that is generally accepted. But another story was and is told by the people of Venice. They, too, claim that they possess the body of Saint Nicholas, and insist that it was taken from Myra by Venetian merchants in the year 1100, and reburied in Venice by the citizens.

They do not accept the story told by the Bari merchants, but declare that the latter carried off from another spot the body of another saint, possibly of the same name, which they palmed off upon their fellow citizens as the body of the former Bishop of Myra.

The true body, they claim, is that which lies to-day, as it has lain for centuries, in the church of St. Nicholas on the Lido. The Lido is a bank of sand which projects, promontory fashion, out of the Grand Canal in Venice into the Adriatic Sea.

The fame of a holy man so closely connected with two great trading ports of the Middle Ages was sure to spread wider and wider among the nations of Europe. And, indeed, we find that everywhere sailors acknowledged him as their special guide and protector and sang his praises wherever they landed.

Both at Bari and at Venice the churches dedicated in his honor stand close to the mouth of the harbor. Venetian crews on their way out to sea would land at the Lido and proceed to the church of St. Nicholas, there to ask for a blessing on their voyage. There also they would stop on their home-coming to give thanks for a safe return. Sailors of Bari would in the same way honor the shrine in which lay what they claimed was the true body of Saint Nicholas.

Many tales of miraculous escapes from shipwreck, due to the intercession of their patron, were related by seamen and travellers, not only at home, but at the various ports where they stopped, so that the name and fame of the good Saint Nicholas grew more resplendent every year. Churches erected in his honor abound in the fishing villages and harbors of Europe.

In England alone, before the Reformation, there were 376 churches which bore his name. The largest parish church in the entire land is that of St. Nicholas at Yarmouth, which was built in the twelfth century and retains that name to the present day. Some of the other churches were rebaptized by the Protestants.

The churches dedicated to Saint Nicholas in Catholic countries are especially dear to people who make their living out of the sea. Sailors and fishermen when ashore frequent them, and if they have just escaped from any of the perils of the deep they show gratitude to their patron by hanging up on the church walls what are known as votive pictures. These are either prints of the saint or sketches, rudely drawn by local artists, which represent the danger that the sail-

ors had run and the manner in which they had escaped.
Often a figure of Saint Nicholas appears in the dark-
ened heavens to calm the fears of the imperilled
mariners.

It is fishermen and sailors also who take the chief
part in the great festival in honor of Saint Nicholas
that is celebrated at Bari on the fifth 'and sixth of
December in every year.

Bari, it may be well to explain, is a very old and
still a very important seaport on the eastern coast of
southern Italy.   It is situated on a small peninsula
projecting into the Adriatic.   From very early days
the city has been the official seat of an archbishop and
hence possesses a grand old cathedral.

Grand, however, as is this cathedral, it is eclipsed
both in beauty and in popular regard by the church
of Saint Nicholas which I have already mentioned
as containing the bones of the saint.   These repose
in a sepulchre, or huge tomb, that stands in a magnificent crypt some twenty feet beneath the high altar.
Water trickles out through the native rock which
forms the tomb.   It is collected by the priests on
a sponge attached to a reed, is squeezed into bottles,
and sold or given away under the name of "Manna
of Saint Nicholas" as a cure for many ailments.

On the eve of Saint Nicholas' Day, that is on the
day before it (December 5th) the city of Bari is
overrun by hosts of pilgrims from the neighboring

cities, as well as others from the furthest corners of Italy and even from Mediterranean France and Spain and Adriatic Austria. All Catholic mariners whose ships happen to be lying in port at the time are sure to join the throng.

The pilgrims carry staffs decorated with olive, palm or pine branches. From each staff depends a water bottle, which is to be filled with the manna of Saint Nicholas. Most of the pilgrims are barefoot. All are clad in the picturesque costumes in use in their native places on holiday occasions.

On entering the church the pilgrims may, if they choose, make a complete circuit of it, moving around on their knees with their foreheads pressed every now and then against the marble pavement. Often a little child leads them by means of a string or handkerchief, one end being held in the mouth of the pilgrim.

Next day, December 6th,—the actual feast of Saint Nicholas,—is celebrated by a procession of the seafaring men of Bari. Rising at daybreak they enter the church early in the morning. The priests, who have assembled to greet them, take down from the altar a wooden image of Saint Nicholas, clad in the robes of a bishop. This is handed over to the care of the paraders for the rest of the day. The priests may accompany the image only as far as the outer gate of the church. The procession, with the image in the hands of its leaders, files out into the street and, fol-

The Christ child surrounded by angels.

Painting by Rubens.

lowed by the populace, visits the cathedral and other sacred or public places.   Then the leaders take Saint Nicholas out to sea in a boat.   Hundreds of other boats accommodate their fellow paraders, as also such of the citizens as can afford the luxury, and follow Saint Nicholas over the waves.

The shore meanwhile is lined with the bulk of the populace of Bari and the pilgrim visitors who eagerly await the return of the image at nightfall.   Bonfires are then burned, rockets are shot off, everybody who possesses a candle or torch lights it and the people fall in line with the paraders to restore the sacred image to its guardians at the church.

CHAPTER III

CHRIST-KINKLE AND CHRIST-KINDLEIN

I HAVE now told you all that is known of the story of Saint Nicholas during his lifetime and even after his death. I think you will agree that we have not yet gone very far in identifying Santa Klaus, the modern Saint Nicholas, with the historic saint who was once Bishop of Myra.

It is true that some learned men have thought to find in the legend of the three maidens an answer to a couple of problems that bother the inquiring mind.

First they explain that the three purses of gold, which, in pictures by the old Italian masters, figure as three golden balls, and which were looked upon as the special symbol or sign of the charitable Saint Nicholas, are the origin of those three gilt balls which swing over a pawnbroker's shop in token of that well-spring of human kindness which has earned for him the affectionate title of "uncle."

If you have a fine sense of humor you will see that the last sentence is sarcasm. And if you have small love for clever explanations that don't explain, you

"Suffer little children to come unto me."

Painting by B. Plockhorst.

will reject this theory of the origin of the pawn-broker's sign and prefer to believe that it sprang from the gilt pills which adorned the shield of the great Medici family of Italy. Medici means doctors. Both the name and the shield were reminders that the family earned their first fame as physicians many years before they became the greatest princes and money changers of Europe.

But the other theory, what of that? The other theory is more to the point. It assumes that the Saint Nicholas who was Bishop of Myra is the Santa Klaus of modern Christmas, whom he pre-figured in the fact that he appeared in the night-time and secretly made valuable presents to the children of a certain household.

Here is some appearance of truth. In the first place there can be no doubt that Santa Klaus and Saint Nicholas are the same name. Indeed to this day our Christmas saint is known either as Santa Klaus or Saint Nicholas, Klaus in Dutch being "short and sweet" for Nicholaus, and, as such, the same as our Nick for Nicholas.

But, after all, there seems to be little likeness in other respects between the saint of the legend and the modern patron of the Christmas season. What connection is there between a single case of charity, performed at no particular time, with the splendid and widespread generosity of Santa Klaus, who every

Christmas eve loads himself down with presents for the little ones he loves, and finds means to distribute them all over the land in a single night?

As the answer is not apparent on the surface, let us turn to the other legend. We shall have to confess however that the story of the three school boys miraculously restored to life after they had been cut up and salted down, helps us even less than does the story of the three purses. It is simply one of a whole group of stories wherein Saint Nicholas appears as the friend and benefactor of children. In this respect only does he resemble our Santa Klaus.

In all the characteristics which modern painters and story tellers, in America, in Holland and in Germany, have bestowed upon the jolly saint of the Christmas season he differs entirely from the slender and even emaciated Nicholas, clad in the robes of a bishop, with a mitre on his head and a crozier in his hand, whom the early painters were fond of depicting.

So the legends of Saint Nicholas afford but a slight clew to the origin of Santa Klaus,—alike, indeed, in name but so unlike in all other respects.

Let us turn elsewhere. In Germany and to a certain extent in America the name Christ-Kinkle or Kriss-Kingle is looked upon as another name for Santa Klaus. But in fact history teaches us that is a far different Being, though the two have been welded into one in the popular imagination.

Christ the giver.
Painting by Murillo.

A very small knowledge of German reveals the fact that Christ-Kinkle is simply a "corruption" or mistaken pronunciation of the German word Christ-Kindlein which in English means Christ child.   Now the connection of the Christ child with the gift-giving season is obvious enough.   In the first place He is the hero of Christmas day itself.   Born a human child He ever preserved a great love, for young people.

"Suffer little children to come unto me," He said, "for of such is the kingdom of Heaven."

The old masters were fond of painting Him as a child among children.   In nearly all the famous pictures which Raphael, the greatest of Italian artists, painted of the Holy Family or of the Madonna and Child, the infant Jesus is accompanied by the infant Saint John as friend and playmate.

CHAPTER IV

Now I must own that at first sight it is difficult to explain how the Christ-child of the past—the Holy One whose birth is remembered and honored in that feast which we call Christmas, should gradually have been changed into the white-haired, white-bearded, merry-hearted and kindly old pagan whom we sometimes call Christ-Kinkle but more frequently Santa Klaus.

Yet at the very moment when we come face to face with this difficult problem we have reached the explanation which seemed impossible when we strove to understand the much less startling transformation of Saint Nicholas, Bishop of Myra, into Santa Klaus, patron of the Christmas season.

We remember that the Christmas festival of to-day is a gradual evolution from times that long antedated the Christian period. We remember that though it celebrates the mightiest event in the history of Christendom, it was overlaid upon heathen festivals, and many of its observances are only adaptations of pagan to Christian ceremonial.

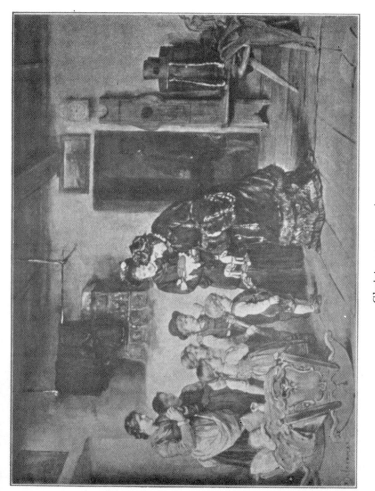

Christmas presents.

Painting by F. Defregger.

This was no mere accident. It was a necessary measure at a time when the new religion was forcing itself upon a deeply superstitious people. In order to reconcile fresh converts to the new faith, and to make the breaking of old ties as painless as possible, these relics of paganism were retained under modified forms, in the same way that antique columns, transferred from pagan temples, became parts of the new churches built by Christians in honor of their God and his saints.

Thus we find that when Pope Gregory sent Saint Augustine as a missionary to convert Anglo-Saxon England he directed that so far as possible the saint should accommodate the new and strange Christian rites to the heathen ones with which the natives had been familiar from their birth. For example, he advised Saint Augustine to allow his converts on certain festivals to eat and kill a great number of oxen to the glory of God the Father, as formerly they had done this in honor of the devil. All pagan gods, it should be explained, were looked upon as devils by the early Christians.

On the very Christmas after his arrival in England Saint Augustine baptized many thousands of converts and permitted their usual December celebration under the new name and with the new meaning. He forbade only the mingling together of Christians and pagans in the dances.

From these early pagan-Christian ceremonies are derived many of the English holiday customs that have survived to our day.

Now get clearly into your head one very important fact. Although at the time when Augustine visited England the date of Christmas had been fixed upon as December 25 there is no biblical reason why this should be so. The gospels say nothing about the season of the year when Christ was born. On the other hand they do tell us that shepherds were then guarding their flocks in the open air. Hence many of the early fathers of the Church considered it most likely that the Nativity took place either in the late summer or the early fall. The point was of no great moment to them, as the early Church made more fuss over the death day of a great or holy person than over his birthday. The birthday is only the day when man is born into mortality, the deathday chronicles his birth into immortality.

The important fact then which I have asked you to get clearly into your head is that the fixing of the date as December 25th was a compromise with paganism.

For countless centuries before the Christian era pagan Europe, through all its various tribes and peoples, had been accustomed to celebrate its chief festival at the time of the winter solstice, the turning point when winter, having reached its apogee, has

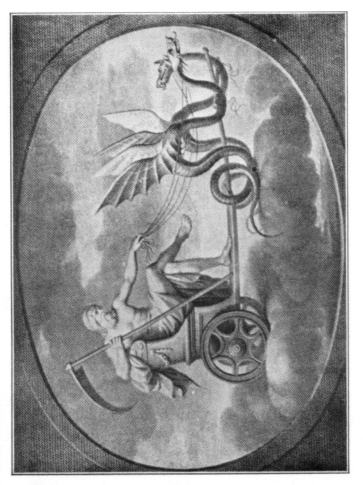

Saturn, the God of Time.
Painting by Raphael.

also reached the point when it must begin to decline again towards spring.

The last sentence requires further explanation. I shall try to put it into words as simple as possible.

You must be aware of the fact that the shortest day in the year is December 21st. Therefore that is the day when winter reaches its height.

It was on or about December 21st that the ancient Greeks celebrated what are known to us as the Bacchanalia or festivities in honor of Bacchus,* the god of wine. In these festivities the people gave themselves up to songs, dances and other revels which frquently passed the limits of decency and order.

In ancient Rome the Saturnalia, or festivals in honor of Saturn, the god of time, began on December 17th and continued for seven days. These also often ended in riot and disorder. Hence the words Bacchanalia and Saturnalia acquired an evil reputation in later times.

We are most interested in the festivals of the ancient Teutonic (or German) tribes because they are most closely linked with Christmas as we ourselves celebrate it.

The pagan feast of the Twelve Nights was religiously kept by them from December 25th to January

---

* Bacchus is the Latin name for this God. The Greek name was Dionysos. This festival therefore is more properly the Dionysiac feast, but the habit of calling Greek Gods by their Roman names is so general among us that it is as well to stick to Bacchus and Bacchanalia.

6th, the latter day being known, as it is still known to their descendants, as Twelfth Night. The Teutonic mind personified the active forces of nature,— that is to say it pictured them as living beings.

The conflicts between these forces were represented as battles between gods and giants.

Winter, for example, was the Ice-giant,—cruel, boisterous, unruly, the destroyer of life, the enemy alike of gods and men. Riding on his steed, the all-stiffening North Wind, he built up for himself great castles of ice. Darkness and death followed in his wake.

But the Sun-god and the South Wind, symbols of light and life, gave battle to the Ice-giant. At last Thor, the god of the Thunderstorm, riding on the wings of the air, hurled his thunderbolt at the winter castle, and demolished it. Then Freija, the goddess of fruits and flowers, resumed her former sway. All of which is only a poetical way of saying that after the Ice-giant had conquered in winter he was in his turn overthrown by the Sun-god in spring.

Now the twenty-first day of December, the depth of winter, marked the period when the Ice-giant was in the full flush of his triumph and also marked the beginning of his overthrow. It was the turning point in the conflict of natural forces. The Sun-god having reached the goal of the winter solstice, now wheeled around his fiery steeds and became the sure herald of the coming victory of light and life over darkness and death of spring over winter.

A thousand indications point to the fact that Christmas has incorporated into itself all these festivals, Greek, Roman and German, and given them a new meaning. The wild revels of the Bacchanalia, the Saturnalia and the Twelve Nights survive in a milder form in the merriment and jollity which mark the season of Christmas to-day.

Christmas gifts themselves remind us of the presents that were exchanged in Rome during the Saturnalia. In Rome, it might be added, the presents usually took the form of wax tapers and dolls,—the latter being in their turn a survival of the human sacrifices once offered to Saturn.

It is a queer thought that in our Christmas presents we are preserving under another form one of the most savage customs of our barbarian ancestors!

The shouts of "Bona Saturnalia!" which the Roman people exchanged among themselves are the precursors of our "Merry Christmas!" The decorations and illuminations of our Christian churches recall the temples of Saturn, radiant with burning tapers and resplendent with garlands. The masks and mummeries which still survive here and there, even in the America of to-day, and which were especially prominent in the Middle Ages, were prominent also in the Saturnalian revels.

And a large number of the legends, superstitions and ceremonials which have crystallized around the Christian festival in Europe and America are more or less distorted reminiscences of the legends, superstitions and ceremonials of the Twelve Nights of ancient Germany.

CHAPTER V

AND now you may be tempted to ask, "What bearing has all this stuff about the pagan festivals upon the question of the identity of our old friend Santa Klaus?

I am coming to that. In every one of these festivals the leading figure was an old man, with a lot of white beard and white hair rimming his face.

In the Bacchanalia the representative god was not the young Bacchus, but the aged, cheery and decidedly disreputable Silenus, the chief of the Satyrs and the god of drunkards.

In the Saturnalia it was Saturn, a dignified and venerable old gentleman—the god of Time.

In the Germanic feasts it was Thor, a person of patriarchal aspect, and a warrior to boot.

Now, although the central figure of the Christian festival was the child-god—the Christ-Kindlein— none the less the influence of long pagan antecedents was too strong within the breast of the newly Christianized world to be readily dismissed. The tradition of hoary age as the true representative of the holiday

69

period, a tradition, it will be seen, in which all pagan nations agreed, still remained smouldering under the ashes of the past. It burst into flame again when the past was too far back to be looked upon with dislike or disquietude by the Church. No longer did there seem to be any danger of a relapse into the religious errors of that past.

At first the more dignified representative was chosen as more in keeping with a solemn season. Saturn was preferred to Silenus, and was almost unconsciously rebaptized as Saint Nicholas, the latter being the greatest saint whose festival was celebrated in December and the one who in other respects was most nearly in accord with the dim traditions of Saturn as the hero of the Saturnalia.

If you look at the pictures printed in this book you will see that in face and figure the Saint Nicholas of the early painters was not unlike the ancient idea of Saturn.

And it was many, many years before Saint Nicholas had ousted the Christ-child from the first place in the Christmas festivities. Indeed, as we shall see, he often accompanied his Master on His Christmas rounds. It may be added that he still does so in certain country places in Europe where the modern spirit has been least felt.

In course of time, as the idea of worldly merriment at the Christmas season prevailed over that of

Silenus and Fauns.

Painting by Annibale Caracci.

prayer and thanksgiving, the name Saint Nicholas gradually merged into the affectionate diminutive of Santa Klaus. Under the new name the old saint lost all his austerity. He became ruddier, jollier, more rubicund in aspect, while the Christ-Kindlein faded more and more into the background, until at last the very name of the latter, under the slightly different form of Kris-Kinkle, was transferred to his successor.

And now compare the pictures of Santa Klaus which are scattered through this book with that of Silenus. Is it not evident that the one is a revival of the other, changed, indeed, in certain traits of character, sobered up, washed and purified, clad in warm garments that are more suited to the wintry season which he has made his own, but still the god of good fellows,—the representative of good health, good humor and good cheer?

Extremes meet once more. The most modern hero of the season of merriment is a return to the most ancient. The Santa Klaus of to-day is the Silenus of an unknown antiquity.

Let us learn a little more about Silenus. He was the tutor of Bacchus and seems to have had so much respect for his pupil that his life after the invention of wine was one long spree. It was a merry and good-natured spree, however. Silenus never became maudlin or quarrelsome in his cups. He was the most jovial of tipplers. His outlook upon life was as rosy as his nose. A cheery laugh beamed over his large fat face, the light of humor twinkled in his beady eyes, his rotund stomach spoke of good cheer, his smile beamed assurance of an unruffled disposition.

Among all the brute creation he chose an ass, that caricature of the horse, as his favorite charger. He always appeared with a troupe of laughing fauns and satyrs around him, and his advent was everywhere the signal for quips and cranks and wreathèd smiles.

Now Saint Nicholas, also, in former times used to ride abroad on an ass, and still continues to do so in certain portions of Europe. In fact, as already noted, all the genial traits of Silenus, save only that of drunkenness, are reproduced in Santa Klaus,—the jolly pagan who is to-day the personification of Christmas.

But though a modernized pagan god holds this important position in our festival, everything that could be offensive in the old pagan way of celebrating it has been abolished.

It was not always so. The Church which so wisely sought to retain the old heathen forms, found it often very hard, and sometimes impossible, to subdue the heathen spirit. In spite of the protests of priests and the anathemas of popes, in spite of the condemnation of all wise and good men, Christians in the early days frequently reproduced all the worst follies and vices

Santa Claus and his young friends.

From Thomas Nast's "Christmas Drawings for the Human Race."
Copyright 1899 by Harper and Brothers.

of the Bacchanalia and the Saturnalia. Even the
clergy were for a period whirled into the vortex. A
special celebration, called the Feast of Fools, was
instituted in their behalf with a view, said the doctors
of the Church, that "the folly which is natural to and
born with us might exhale at least once a year." The
intention was excellent. But in practice the liberty
so accorded speedily degenerated into license.

Early in the history of the Church excesses were
so great that a council of bishops held at Auxerre
was moved to inquire into the matter. Gerson, the
most noted theologian of the day, made an immense
sensation by declaring that "if all the devils in hell
had put their heads together to devise a feast that
should utterly scandalize Christianity, they could not
have improved upon this one."

If even among the clergy heathen traditions survived so strenuously, what wonder that they survived
among the laity? The wild revels, indeed, of the
Christmas period in olden times almost stagger belief.
No amount of drunkenness, no blasphemy, no ob-
scenity was frowned upon. License was carried to
the utmost limits of licentiousness. Even in the
seventeenth century, when the revels had been slightly
toned down, Master William Prynne discovered in
them those vestiges of paganism which are apparent
enough to the historian of to-day.

"If we compare," he says in his *Histrio-Mastix,*

"our Bacchanalian Christmas and New Year's tides
with these Saturnalia and feasts of Janus, we shall
find such near affinity between them, both in regard
of time,—they being both in the end of December
and the first of January—and in their manner of sol-
emnizing—both being spent in revelling, epicurism,
wantonness, idleness, dancing, drinking, stage-plays,
masques and carnal pomp and jollity—that we must
conclude the one to be but the ape, or issue, of the
other."

The very excesses of the Christmas period proved
their own eventual cure. In England the Puritans
revolted so bitterly that they for a period put an end
to Christmas altogether. In Europe the revolution
was more gradual. But everywhere a change of manners and of morals has purified the festival over which
Santa Klaus presides, and Santa Klaus himself, even
if we look upon him as a revival of the pagan Silenus,
is a Silenus freed from all the offensive features of
paganism, a Silenus who with his new baptismal name
has taken on a new character.

It must be remembered, however, that Santa Klaus
does not rule all over the Christian world. There is
even a wide difference between our Santa Klaus and
the Saint Nicholas of Southern France and Germany.
The latter, grave, sedate, severe, preserves more of
the Saturn than the Silenus type. He is Saturn
christianized and dignified with episcopal robes. He

Carrying home the Christmas dinner.

Drawing by John Leech.

distributes gifts like our Santa Klaus, but in addition to gifts for good little boys and girls, he carries a birch-rod for bad ones.   In the more primitive sections, such as certain parts of Lorraine, the Tyrol, Bohemia and so on, he is attended by an evil spirit called Ruprecht who looks after bad boys and girls.

It is also frequently the custom on Christmas Day for a couple or more of maskers to dress themselves up as Saint Nicholas and Ruprecht, and other attendants, such as the Christ-child or St. Peter or who not,—these additional characters varying with the locality.   They go from house to house rewarding the good children and punishing the bad.

More of this, however, in a future chapter.

CHAPTER VI

A TERRIBLE CHRISTMAS IN OLD FRANCE

FOREVER memorable as an illustration of the manners of the French court in the fourteenth century stands a terrible accident that happened in Paris on the Christmas eve of 1393. All through the Christmas ceremonies of the preceding week riot had run unchecked. The wildest spirits of the French court had been given a free rein. One mad prank had followed another, until it might seem that imagination had been exhausted in the effort at inventing new follies.

But this would have been reckoning without Sir Hugonin de Guisay. Sir Hugonin was known as the maddest of the mad. The reckless and the ungodly loved and admired him as much as the sober and the godly hated and despised him. From his height as a nobleman of the French court he looked down with contempt on "the common people,"—tradesmen, mechanics, laborers and servants. He found a cruel pleasure in accosting harmless folk of this sort in the public streets, pricking them with his spurs, lashing them with his whip, and ordering them

The Feast of the Passover.
Painting by Diedrich Bouts.

to creep on their hands and feet in the gutters.

"Bark, dog, bark!" he would cry as he cracked his whip in the air.

To please him the victims had to bow-wow and growl like curs ere this polite and pleasant gentleman would allow them to rise from their degraded position.

On this particular Christmas Eve Sir Hugonin had a proposal to make. He suggested that, in order to continue the festivities, a mock marriage should be celebrated between a gentleman and a lady of the court. The proposal was accepted with shouts of joy. A young couple were chosen to stand up before a pretended priest, and to go through the form of the wedding service.

Just as the ceremony was nearing its end Sir Hugonin asked the king and four of his courtiers,— madcaps all of them and all of them members of the proudest families in France,—to withdraw with him for a moment. He had a fresh proposal to make. It happened that at this time all Paris had gone wild over the dancing bears brought into the capital by strolling performers. Hugonin's plan was that he and the king, and the four courtiers, should disguise themselves as dancing bears. A pot of tar and a quantity of tow were ready at hand to transform them into fair imitations of the bears in the players' booths. Then the five courtiers were to be bound together with a silk rope. The king himself would lead them into the hall.

"Excellent!" cried the king and all the courtiers, save only Sir Evan de Foix.

Sir Evan seems to have been the one man of the party who had preserved a glimmer of common sense. He pointed out that they were about to rush into a room full of lights. Being all bound together, no one could say what disaster might not befall.

"Sire," he pleaded, "it is certain that if one of us catches fire, the whole number, including your Majesty, will be as so many roast chestnuts."

Then up spoke the reckless Sir Hugonin. "Who is to set us on fire?" he asked. "Where is there the traitor that would not be careful when the safety of the king is at stake?"

Sir Evan's fears could not be set at rest. But when he found that the counsels of Sir Hugonin were bound to prevail he suggested that at least all due precautions should be taken.

"Let His Majesty be prevailed upon at least to give orders that nobody bearing a torch shall approach us."

"That shall be done at once," said Charles. Instantly sending for the chief officer in charge of the hall he gave instructions that all the torch bearers should be collected together on one side of the room, and that under no pretence should any of them approach a party of savage men who were about to enter and perform a dance. These orders having been given the dancers entered.

They were greeted with a roar of laughter and cheers. The mimic bears followed their leader around the hall saluting the ladies as they passed them; and leaping and dancing for the amusement of the crowd.

"Who are they?" cried the spectators, eager to penetrate the disguise.

Now just at this moment it unfortunately happened that the Duke of Orleans made his appearance at the doors of the hall. He knew nothing of what had been going on behind the scenes. He was attended by six torchbearers, who in obedience to orders, should not have been admitted into the dance-hall. But the Duke of Orleans was the king's brother. It was hard to dictate to the first prince of the blood. He could scarcely be included in any general order. So he was allowed to pass in with his companions.

"Who are they?" he exclaimed, taking up the cry that was ringing around the hall. "Well, we shall soon find out."

Snatching a brand from one of his torchbearers he peered into the faces of the dancers, seeking to identify them. Coming at last to Sir Evan de Foix, he shouted out his name, and caught him by the arm. Sir Evan tried to shake himself free. But the Duke would not loosen his hold. Just then some one jostled his elbows and the torch he held in his hand was brought into sudden contact with the tarry tow that did duty as a bearskin. In one moment Sir Evan was blazing from head to foot. In another moment the whole group of knights were aflame. Their frantic struggles served only to draw them more closely together within the silken rope that bound them.

Luckily for the king he had detached himself from the group, having stopped on his rounds to talk to the Duchess de Berri. When first the alarm was given he would have rushed to help his companions, but the duchess, guessing it was the king under this disguise, threw her arms around him and forcibly detained him.

"Sire," she said, "do you not see that your companions are burning to death, and that nothing could save you if you went near them in that dress?"

Meanwhile, one of the maskers had wrenched himself free from his companions. This was the young Lord of Nantouillet, famous for strength, agility and presence of mind, possessed, moreover, of a powerful jaw and a splendid set of teeth. He bit through the silken rope that enmeshed him, wrenched it off, and then rushed through the hall and flung himself, like a blazing comet, through a window that opened into the yard below. Luckily he had remembered that underneath the window stood a cistern full of water. Plunging headlong into this impromptu bathtub

The Adoration of the Lamb.
Painting by Hubert and Jan Van Eyck.

he emerged, black, burnt and sizzling, but saved.

As for his companions, they were now whirling hither and thither through a horrified mob of spectators, who trampled over each other in their eagerness to escape contact with the blaze. Shrieking, praying, cursing, the doomed four fought with the flames and with one another. Women fainted; men who had never faltered in the fiercest battle sickened at the frightful spectacle. Eager as they would have been to assist their friends, the men knew only too well that no human arm could offer assistance.

All Paris had been aroused by the tumult and now crowded around the palace gates. At last the flames burned out. The four maskers lay, a charred and writhing heap, upon the floor of the dance-hall. One was a mere cinder. Another survived until daybreak. Still another died at noon the next day. The fourth lived on through three days of agony. This was Sir Hugonin himself.

Small pity did he get from the mechanics and tradesmen of Paris!

"Bark, dog, bark!" was the cry with which they greeted the charred and mangled corpse when it was borne through the streets to its final resting place in the cemetery.

CHAPTER VII

THE CHRISTMAS TREE IN LEGEND

WE have seen that most of the ceremonies that have attended or still attend the season of Christmas may be traced back to a period long before the birth of Christ.

The Christmas tree is no exception to this rule. It is pagan, not Christian in its origin, though it has been adapted to Christian uses. It came down to us from the pagan Teutons and Scandinavians, and on the way it was Christianized in Germany and Holland, in Sweden, Norway and Denmark, long before it had been made holy in the same manner among the English-speaking peoples.

Myth and history have both busied themselves with guesses at its origin. Let us begin with myth.

A very old legend makes Saint Winfred the inventor of the Christmas tree. Winfred (please note that this is the masculine form of which Winifred is the feminine) was one of the early missionaries to Norway who helped to wean the ancient Scandinavians from their pagan beliefs and practices.

90

He found that their priests, the Druids, had taught them to worship trees as if they were living gods. So he set himself the task of showing to his Christian converts that the objects of their former worship were not gods but trees,—trees and nothing more. On Christmas eve, therefore, he hewed down a mighty oak in presence of a great crowd of men, women and children.

A miracle indeed followed. But it was a Christian miracle, and as such was all the more convincing to these simple people that their old-time faiths had been misplaced.

This is how the miracle is described by an ancient historian:

"As the bright blade circled around Winfred's head, and the flakes of wood flew from the deepening gash in the body of the tree, a whirling wind passed over the forest. It gripped the oak from its foundations. Backward it fell like a tower, groaning as it split asunder in four pieces. But just behind it and unharmed by the ruin, stood a young fir tree pointing a green spire towards the stars.

"Winfred let the axe drop and turned to speak to the people.

" 'This little tree, a young child of the forest, shall be your holy tree to-night. It is the wood of peace, for your houses are built of the fir. It is a sign of endless life, for its leaves are ever green. See how it points upward to heaven. Let this be called the tree of the Christ-child; gather about it, not in the wildwood, but in your own homes; there it will shelter no deeds of blood, but loving gifts and rites of kindness.' "

There is another old legend that is told by the people around Strassburg, a famous old city on the Rhine. Half way between this city and the neighboring town of Drusenheim there are still to be seen the ruins of an old castle. It probably dates back to the seventh century. Its chief feature is a massive gate. Deep sunk in the stone arch above this gate, and as clearly and sharply defined as if it had been carved only yesterday, is the impress of a small and delicate hand. And this is the story that is told to account for the presence of the hand.

One of the early lords of the castle was Count Otto von Gorgas, a handsome and dashing youth, whose great delight was hunting big game. So devoted, indeed, was he to the shooting of deer and the spearing of wild boars that love could find no entrance into his heart. In vain did the fairest maidens in the land sigh for a soft speech or a tender glance from this wild huntsman. Mothers on both banks of the river Rhine had abandoned in despair all hope of securing him as a match for their daughters, while the daughters themselves had spitefully given him the name of Stony-heart, by which he had become generally known throughout the country side.

But Count Otto only laughed at the anger of the ladies, and continued to kill with his own hand such large quantities of game that new servants would not come into his employ, unless he had first agreed to give them venison or wild boar steaks not oftener than four days in the week.

One Christmas Eve Count Otto ordered that a battue or monster hunt should take place in the forest surrounding his castle. So exciting was the sport that he was led deep into the thickets and at night-fall found himself separated from all his friends and followers. He reined up beside a far-away spring, clear and deep, known to the country people as the Fairy's Well. His hands being stained with the blood of the wild animals he had slain, he dismounted from his horse to wash them in the spring.

Though the weather was cold and a white frost covered the dead leaves, Count Otto found to his surprise that the water of the well was warm and pleasant. A delightful feeling ran through his veins. Plunging his arms deeper into the well, he fancied that he felt his right hand grasped by another hand softer and smaller than his own, which gently drew from his finger a gold ring that he was accustomed to wear.

Sure enough, when he pulled his hand out of the water the ring was gone!

Though annoyed by his loss, the count decided that the ring had accidentally slipped from his finger. There was no opportunity for any further search that day, for the well was very deep and the sun had already set.

So Otto remounted his horse and rode back to the castle, resolving that in the morning he would have the Fairy's Well emptied out by his servants. Little doubt had he but that the ring would easily be found at the bottom.

As a rule Count Otto was a good sleeper. That night, however, he tried in vain to close his eyes. Lying restlessly awake he listened feverishly to the hoarse baying of the watch-dog in the court-yard until near midnight. Suddenly he raised himself on his elbows. What was that unusual noise he heard outside?

He strained his ears. Distinctly he again heard the creaking of the drawbridge as it was being lowered. A few minutes later there followed sounds as of the pattering of many feet up the stone stairs and into the chamber next to his own. Then a wild strain of music came floating on the air, shooting a sweet mysterious thrill even into his "stony" heart.

Rising softly from his bed, Otto hastily dressed himself. A little bell sounded. His chamber door was suddenly flung open. He accepted what seemed like a wordless invitation. Crossing the threshold into the next room, he found himself in the midst of an assemblage of rather small but very lovely looking strangers of both sexes, who laughed, chatted, danced and sang without seeming in the least to notice him.

In the middle of the room stood a splendid Christmas tree from which a great number of many-colored lamps shed a flood of light throughout the apartment.

Now this was the first Christmas tree that had ever been seen in those parts, or indeed by any mortal folk in any portion of the world. And it was a Christmas tree of a sort that never again has been seen by any mortal folk in any portion of the world.

For surely never again has a Christmas tree borne such fruits. Instead of toys and candies the branches were hung with diamond stars and crosses, pearl necklaces, aigrettes of rubies and sapphires, baldricks embroidered with Oriental pearls, and daggers mounted in gold and studded with the rarest gems.

Lost in wonder at a scene he could not understand, the count gazed without the power of uttering a single word. There was a sudden movement at the end of the hall. The company stopped dancing and fell back to make way for a newcomer. Then in the bright rays of the Christmas lights, a dazzling vision stood in front of Count Otto.

It was a princess of astonishing beauty. Though only a girl in size, she was a woman in age. Though small, her body was exquisitely formed. There she stood, magnificently dressed as for a ball. A diadem sparkled amid her raven black locks, rich point lace only half veiled her snowy bosom, and her dress of rose-colored silk sat close to her slender figure, falling in folds just so low as to reveal the neatest feet and ankles in the world, while her sleeves were short enough to display beautiful arms of dazzling whiteness.

The charming stranger showed no awkward timidity. On the contrary, after a short pause she walked straight up to the count, caught him by both hands, and said, in the sweetest of voices:

"Dear Otto, I am come to return your call."

At the same time she raised her right hand to his lips. Forgetting all his old coldness towards the female sex he gallantly kissed it without making any other reply. Indeed, he felt fascinated, spellbound. He gladly let the beautiful stranger draw him to a couch where she sat herself down besides him. Her lips met his and before he could think about kissing them, he had done so.

"My dear friend," whispered the lady into his ear, "I am the fairy Ernestine. I have brought you a Christmas present. That which you lost and hardly hoped to find again, see! I fetch it back to you."

And, drawing from her bosom a little casket set with diamonds, she placed it in the hands of the count. He eagerly opened it. Not entirely unexpectedly (for had not her words forewarned him?) he found within it the ring that he had lost in the forest well.

Carried away by a feeling as strange as it was irresistible, Count Otto pressed the casket and then the lovely Ernestine to his breast.

"Delightful," murmured the maiden, who as you may see, was not so coy as are many maidens of the everyday world.

In brief the two had fallen in love with each other at first sight. Before they parted for the night, Otto had won the fairy's consent to become his wife.

One thing only she demanded of him. He must never make use of the word "death" in her presence. Fairies are immortal; she did not wish to be reminded that she was bound to a mortal husband.

It was easy enough for him to make this promise, and no doubt he thought it would be easy to keep it. Next day Count Otto von Gorgas and Ernestine, the Queen of the Fairies, were married with great pomp and ceremony. They lived happily together for some years in the grand old castle.

One day it chanced that the young couple were to assist at a great tourney in the neighborhood. The Lady Ernestine's horse stood in waiting for her at the castle gate. Being greatly occupied in adjusting a new headdress which her milliner had just brought home, she kept her husband waiting until his patience was worn out.

"Fair dame," he pettishly exclaimed when she at last appeared in the great hall where for half an hour he had been striding up and down in his uncomfortable armor, "you are so long making ready, you would be a good messenger to send for Death."

Scarcely had he uttered the fatal word than with a wild scream the lady disappeared. She left no trace behind her, except the print of her little hand above the castle gate. Every Christmas eve, however, she returns and flits about the ruins with loud lamentations, crying at intervals:

"Death! Death! Death!"

As to Count Otto he went the way of all flesh and was gathered to his fathers not long after he had lost his spouse. But every Christmas Eve, while his life lasted, he would set up a lighted tree in the hall where he had first met the lady Ernestine,—in the vain hope of wooing her back to his arms. And this, it is said in Strasburg and its neighborhood, was the origin of the Christmas tree.*

* London Illustrated News, December 25, 1858. Schulzer: Legends of the Rhine.

CHAPTER VIII

THE stories I have just told you are pretty enough and may amuse an idle half hour. But we must now pass from the region of myth into that of history and science.

My sexagenarian readers will not need to be introduced to the science called comparative mythology. But for the sake of the six year olds it may be well to explain, as simply as I can in a few words, that comparative mythology is a branch of human knowledge which compares the myths and legends of one age and one people with the myths and legends of another age and another people, the object being to show how the later myths descend from the earlier ones, or how all the myths go back to some parent germ in the far-a-way past.

By the aid, then, of the science of comparative mythology let us seek to study the historical growth of the idea that is now embodied in the Christmas tree. Here, indeed, we are in a whirl of problems. Comparative mythology is one of the most interesting and also one of the most difficult of sciences. In the present case it must take account of the fact that we English speaking peoples of the present day, and especially we Americans, are a hodge-podge mixture of many races and many religions. Somewhere in our brains we preserve dim memories of a thousand conflicting myths of the past which without knowing it we have inherited from our ancestors. In other parts of our brain we retain the facts and fictions which have been told to us by our elders, or which we have learned from books.

Now in all times and in all countries we find records of the worship, at some former period, of a tree as a divinity,—in other words as a god.

Greatest and most famous of all these sacred trees was a quite imaginary one which the Scandinavians called the ash-tree Yggdrasil. Nobody had ever seen it, but everybody among these imaginative people believed in its existence.

It was supposed to be a tree so big that you could not possibly picture it to your fancy, which encompassed the entire universe of sun and moon and stars and earth. And it had three roots, one in heaven, one in hell and one on earth.

The serpent who gnaws the roots of Yggdrasil was of course a heathen idea. Yet you cannot help seeing in him some likeness to the serpent of Genesis who is held to be a symbol of Satan, or the devil. Like Satan he seeks the destruction of the universe.

Luther and the Christmas tree.

When the roots of Yggdrasil are eaten through the tree will fall over and the end of all things will have arrived.

Now among the Anglo-Saxons or early inhabitants of England, who were in part descended from the Scandinavians, Yggdrasil survived in the Yule log. which they used to burn on Christmas Eve, as it is still burned in many an English home to-day.

And this is how the pagan tree was transformed into the Christian Yule log:—

The missionaries to the Anglo-Saxons denounced the Yggdrasil superstition. They made their converts hack to pieces all carved figures representing the idolatrous symbol, and then cast the pieces into the flames as a token that the Christ-child had destroyed heathenism.

Among the Germans and the Norsemen, however, the sanctity of the Yggdrasil myth could not be destroyed. It had to be transformed, and transferred to Christian uses by identifying it with some Christian or Jewish symbol like the tree of life in Genesis or the cross of Christ in the New Testament.

Compare the great tree Yggdrasil and its three roots with the description which a certain writer of the early middle ages, called Alcima, gives of the Tree of Life.

"It's position," says Alcima, "is such that the upper

portion touches the earth, the root reaches to hell,
and the branches extend to all parts of the earth."

Evidently Alcima had been influenced by Scandi-
navian legend as well as by biblical lore. Of course
you will understand that he was speaking not of the
actual cross, but of the cross as a symbol of Christianity.

Let us extend our researches a little further into
the region of comparative mythology.

You will find Adam and Eve commemorated in
old calendars under date of December 24th. This
is the eve of Christmas. The symbol of our first parents is the tree of the knowledge of good and evil.
Christmas itself is the day of Christ, whose symbol
is the tree of life or the cross. It is easy to see that
when the minds of men were escaping from paganism
into Christianity the tree of the old mythology grew
to be associated with the birthday of Christ and thus
with the cross. So the lights of the Chanuckah Festival of the Hebrews were borrowed to adorn the
sacred tree, and the seven-branched candlestick, as
a figure of that tree, was even introduced into the
churches.

The representation—so common among the early
painters and especially the painters of Italy—of the
serpent squatting at the foot of the cross had of course
its Christian meaning, but its adoption into Christian

art was in great degree influenced by the fact that
the cross had become popularly identified with the
serpent tree of the old pagan myth.

Scandinavia was not the only place that had its
sacred tree. Egypt, for instance, had one in the palm,
which puts forth a shoot every month. A spray of
this tree with twelve shoots on it was used in ancient
Egypt at the time of the winter solstice as a symbol
of the twelvemonth or completed year.

From Egypt the custom reached Rome, where
it was added to the other ceremonies of the Saturnalia.
But as palm trees do not grow in Italy other trees
were used in its stead. A small fir tree, or the crest
of a large one was found to be the most suitable,
because it is shaped like a cone or a pyramid. This
was decorated with twelve burning tapers lit in honor
of the god of Time. At the very tip of the pyramid
blazed the representation of a radiant sun placed there
in honor of Apollo, the sun-god, to whom the three
last days of December were dedicated. These days
were called the sigillaria, or seal-days, because presents were then made of impressions stamped on wax.

In further honor of Apollo, who was a shepherd
in his youth, images of sheep were shown pasturing
under the tree. Apollo himself sometimes took
charge of the herd, or taught the shepherds the use
of the musical pipe. All these customs were skilfully
adapted by the priests of the early Church to Chris-

tian uses. Shepherd and sheep were retained as symbols of Christ and his flock. As you know, our Lord is frequently alluded to as the good shepherd and is so represented in religious paintings. The sigillaria of the old Romans were also turned to a new use, the wax being now stamped with figures of saints and other holy persons.

A few pages back you were told that the day before Christmas is the day which our pious forefathers dedicated to Adam and Eve. Hence, you will remember, figures of our first parents appeared at the foot of the tree, while a serpent entwined itself around the roots or the trunk. This was the serpent of the Old Testament, but I have already explained how it was also a Christian adaptation of the serpent of the great ash-tree Yggdrasil.

I may add, right here, that the serpent still makes its appearance at the base of a Christmas tree in many parts of rural Germany where old customs still survive in their original purity.

And now by grouping all these facts together we find that long before the coming of Christ there was scattered all over the world an idea that an illuminated tree was a symbol of holiness. Therefore it was only natural that it came at last to be associated with the birthday of Christ and with the period of the winter solstice which the followers of Christ had rescued from pagan practices and pagan superstitions and adapted to the religion which He had founded.

This association was made all the more natural because the candles that twinkle on the Christmas tree were anticipated in the candles lit by the Jews on their Chanuckah or Feast of Lights. Chanuckah is still celebrated among them with all the old forms. It falls on the twenty-fifth day of Kislev, or ninth month of the Jewish calendar, which roughly corresponds with our December or twelfth month.

On that day, in the year 165 before Christ, the temple in Jerusalem, which had been desecrated by a Roman army under Antiochus, had been purified and rededicated by Judas Maccabeus. Antiochus had put out the lights of the seven-branched candelabra that had been kept burning ever since the temple had been finished. A jar of sacred oil, sealed with the ring of the High Priest, was discovered untouched. There seemed to be only enough for one day but when it was poured into the lamp it lasted for a full week. This miracle happened just in the nick of time, for it would have taken seven days to obtain a fresh supply of oil. It was then decreed that the week beginning with the twenty-fifth day of Kislev should be celebrated as a festival forever.

Accordingly on that day in every year the Jews light a candle in every home, on the next day, two, and so on, until the seventh and last day of the feast when seven candles twinkle in every home.

Now if Christ was born on the twenty-fifth day of December he probably came into the world at a time when every house in Bethlehem and Jerusalem was ablaze with lights.

In this connection it may be added that one of the German names for Christmas is Weinacht or Night of Dedication, as though it were somehow associated in the popular mind with the Jewish Chanuckah. Another curious fact which bears out the same theory is that the Catholics of the Greek Church call Christmas the Feast of Lights.

With another Jewish festival Christmas has a verbal link. This is the feast of the Passover when a lamb is killed and eaten. Christ is often symbolized as a lamb. Saint John the Baptist, you remember, greeted him as "the Lamb of God who taketh away the sins of the world."

CHAPTER IX

WE have now considered the far-off origins of the Christmas tree. We have decided that it is an adaptation of the Yggdrasil and other sacred trees of the pagan past to Christian and modern uses. Not yet, however, have we bridged the chasm that divides the history of the old tree from that of the new one.

How, where and by whom was the Christmas tree, as we now know it, brought into the Christmas festivities and associated with the Christ-child and Saint Nicholas? I am sorry to say that it is impossible to give positive answers to any of these questions.

There is, indeed, a very popular German tradition which makes Martin Luther the inventor of the modern Christmas tree. One bright Christmas eve, it is said, as Luther was journeying home through a snow-covered country, he was more than ever struck by the wondrous spectacle of the star-lit sky above him.

It is a very common saying, one which dates back to an old Greek philosopher but which has been repeated by many other wise men of modern times,

that if a grown person who had all his life gone to
bed with the setting sun and got up with the rising
one, and who, therefore, had never seen the moon or
the stars, were suddenly to be awakened at midnight,
he would be overwhelmed by the glorious mystery
of the spectacle overhead. We who are accustomed
to the sight from our cradles can hardly realize the
shock of such a surprise. Because we have seen
the moon and stars ever since we could remember
we forget how wonderful they are, and how beautiful
is the scene they present. We take them as a matter
of course.

Now Martin Luther was a poet as well as a
preacher. One great difference between a poet and
an ordinary person of slower imagination is that he
adds to the wisdom of manhood the freshness and
simplicity of childhood. He retains the young heart
with the mature brain. As Carlyle, a great modern
writer, has said, he sees the world "rimmed around
with wonder." Carlyle being, like Martin Luther, a
poet, even though he rarely put his thoughts into
verse and rhyme, never lost the sense of wonder and
awe towards the manifestations of God in the universe.

God is everywhere, though we poor, purblind
folk only now and then catch glimpses of Him. If
we could clear away the mists that have gathered
round our eyes during our progress through the world

Christmas tree of the English royal family.
From the "Illustrated London News," December, 1842.

we would know that He is everywhere. It is the poet who keeps his eyes clearest for the Blessed Vision.

Luther arrived at home, so the story continues, with brain and heart full of the feelings and the thoughts that had been inspired in him by the firmament of shining stars. He tried to explain to his wife and children just what those thoughts and feelings were. Suddenly an idea struck him. Going into the garden he cut off a little fir tree, dragged it into the nursery, put some candles into its branches and lighted them. Ever after that, we are told, Luther fixed up a Christmas tree in his home for the instruction and entertainment of his wife and children. The custom was imitated by his neighbors and finally spread all over Germany.

This is a very pretty legend, but it is legend and not history. It deserves no more credit than the story of St. Winfred which I have quoted from German folklore, or the fairy tale which, as I have said, still lingers among the people in and around Strasburgh.

All that we know from real history is that a tree with lighted candles was now and then used in the middle ages, and later, in connection with the Christmas rejoicings.

Such a tree is known to have played its part in a Christmas pageant given at the court of Henry VIII.

in England. The tree is described at some length in the chronicles of the time, but it is evident from these descriptions that it lacked the chief feature of the modern one. It was not a bearer of presents.

So far as it is possible to gather from history, the Christmas tree, as we know it to-day, made its first appearance in Strassburgh. This is interesting in view of the fact that one of the earliest legends in explanation of the custom finds its home in that city. More authentic witness is afforded by an old manuscript still preserved in a library at Friedburg, Germany, which was written by a citizen of Strassburgh in the year 1608. This manuscript speaks of a tree all alight with candles and bedecked with presents as being a regular feature of the Christmas festivities of that time. Therefore we are sure that the Christmas tree had come into common use in this region by the beginning of the seventeenth century. Further than that there is no certainty.

The custom appears to have spread from Strassburgh to the neighboring cities along the Rhine and to have flourished in that limited district for fully two hundred years.

Suddenly, about the beginning of the nineteenth century, it made its appearance outside of the Rhenish towns in other nearby localities, until finally it had invaded the whole of Germany. Fifty years later it had conquered nearly all Christendom.

In the year 1825 the English poet, Samuel Taylor Coleridge, visited Germany to spend the winter months in that country.   One of his letters written in the following January speaks of the Christmas tree as something entirely unknown to his fellow countrymen.

"There is a Christmas custom here," he says, "which pleased and interested me.   The children make little presents to their parents and to each other and the parents to their children.   For three or four months before Christmas the girls are all busy and the boys save up their pocket money to buy these presents.   What the present is to be is cautiously kept secret; and the girls have a world of contrivances to conceal it—such as working when they are out on visits, and the others are not with them; getting up in the morning before daylight and so forth.   Then, on the evening before Christmas day, one of the parlors is lighted up by the children, into which the parents must not go; a great yew-bough is fastened on the table at a little distance from the wall, a multitude of little tapers are fixed in the bough, but not so as to burn it till they are nearly consumed, and colored paper, etc., hangs and flutters from the twigs.

"Under this bough the children lay out, in great order, the presents they mean for their parents, still concealing in their pockets what they intend for each other.   Then the parents are introduced and each presents his little gift; they then bring out the remainder, one by one, from their pockets, and present them with kisses and embraces. Where I witnessed this scene, there were eight or nine children, and the oldest daughter and the mother wept aloud for joy and tenderness; and the tears ran down the face of the father, and he clasped all his children so tight to his breast, it seemed as if he did it to stifle the sob that was rising within it. I was very much affected. The shadow of the bough and its appendages on the wall, and arching over on the ceiling, made a pretty picture; and then the raptures of the very little ones, when at last the twigs and their needles began to take fire and snap—O! it was a delight to them!

"On the next day (Christmas day) in the great parlor, the parents lay out on the table the presents for the children; a scene of more sober joy succeeds; as on this day, after an old custom, the mother says privately to each of her daughters and the father to his sons, that which he has observed most praiseworthy and that which was most faulty in their conduct."

Continuing, Coleridge tells us that formerly, and still in all the smaller towns and villages throughout North Germany, these presents were sent by all the parents to some young fellows, who, in high buskins, a white robe, a mask, and an enormous flax wig personates Knecht Ruprecht, i. e. the servant Rupert.

"On Christmas night he goes round to every house, and says that Jesus Christ, his Master, sent him thither. The parents and elder children receive him with great pomp and reverence, while the little ones are most terribly frightened. He then inquires for the children, and according to the character which he hears from the parents, he gives them the intended presents, as if they came out of heaven from Jesus Christ, or if they should have been bad children, he gives the parents a rod, and, in name of his Master, recommends them to use it frequently. About seven or eight years old, the children are let into the secret, and it is curious how faithfully they keep it."

CHAPTER X

Coleridge's letter, as we have seen, was written in January 1826. In the succeeding December the English people were to obtain a nearer view of the Christmas tree. A great German lady, the Princess Lieven, who had taken up her residence for a season in London brought many German customs with her.

"On Christmas," says Henry Greville, an amusing gossip whose diary was published after his death, "the Princess Lieven got up a little fête such as is customary all over Germany. Three trees, in great pots, were put upon a long table covered with pink linen. Each tree was illuminated with three circular tiers of colored wax candles,—blue, green, red and white. Before each tree was displayed a quantity of toys, gloves, pocket-handkerchiefs, work boxes, books and various articles—presents made to the owner of the tree. It was very pretty. Here it was only for the children. In Germany the custom extends to persons of all ages."

Not yet, however, did the custom pass over to England. The people who saw the tree in the parlor of the Princess Lieven or who heard about it from those who had there seen it, made no attempt to copy it in their own homes. A dozen years were to pass before the tree took firm roots in English soil.

It was the marriage of Queen Victoria to a German prince—Albert of Saxe-Coburg—that brought about this result. The first child was a daughter (named Victoria after her mother) who became Empress of Germany and the mother of the present Emperor William. The second child was a son, who is now King Edward VII of England. When the Princess Victoria was about five years old Prince Albert set up a Christmas tree, German fashion, in the royal nursery at Windsor Castle.

A writer in the *Cornhill Magazine* places the date of the introduction of the Christmas tree into England as December 1841. He remembers, he says, when his parents, "who had spent many winters in Germany, first introduced it, some forty-five years ago into England, what astonishment it created, what surprised delight it afforded."

This writer gives a little too much credit to his parents. No mere subjects of the queen could have made other people follow so readily in their footsteps. The royal example, however, was sufficient. Once a Christmas tree had been set up in Windsor Castle, you may be sure that Christmas trees blazed and twinkled in every British household that could afford one.   It has remained ever since just what it is with us,—the centre of all the Christmas festivities.

From the *London News* for December, 1848, I have taken a picture which represents the Windsor Castle Christmas tree with the English royal family of that date grouped around it.   It is interesting to note how this English paper deals with the novelty recently brought over from Germany.

"The tree employed for this festive purpose," says the *News*, "is a young fir about eight feet high, and has six tiers of branches.   On each tier, or branch, are arranged a dozen wax tapers.   Pendent from the branches are elegant trays, baskets, *bonbonnières*, and other receptacles for sweetmeats, of the most varied and expensive kind; and of all forms, colours, and degrees of beauty.   Fancy cakes, gilt gingerbread and eggs filled with sweetmeats, are also suspended by variously-coloured ribbons from the branches.   The tree, which stands upon a table covered with white damask, is supported at the root by piles of sweets of a larger kind, and by toys and dolls of all descriptions, suited to the youthful fancy, and to the several ages of the interesting scions of Royalty for whose gratification they are displayed.   The name of each recipient is affixed to the doll, bonbon, or other present intended for it, so that no difference of opinion in the choice of dainties may arise to disturb the equanimity of the illustrious juveniles.   On the summit of the tree stands the small figure of an angel, with outstretched wings, holding in each hand a wreath."

The tree, we are further told, was an object of much interest to all visitors at Windsor Castle from

Christmas Eve, when it was first set up, until Twelfth
Night, when it was taken down. Other trees were
placed in other rooms of the castle. Prince Albert
had his, which was decorated and hung with presents
by Queen Victoria, who in her turn received a tree
furnished in the same manner by her consort.

Two trees also stood on the sideboard of the royal
dining room and presented, we are told, "a brilliant
appearance when all the tapers are lighted up among
the branches."

In America the Christmas tree had become a fixture
long before its appearance in England. German em-
igrants to our shores had brought it over with them,
just as in earlier times the Dutch settlers of New
York had brought over Santa Klaus. But it flourished in German settlements alone for many years
before it was adopted by their neighbors, the northern
descendants of the English Puritans and Pilgrims,
or the southern descendants of the English Cavaliers.

New York, as the great landing place for emi-
grants and also as a city whose Dutch begin-
nings had given it a leaning towards the Teutonic
spirit, was the first spot in which the German Christmas tree made a new home for itself. Gradually but
surely the custom spread to citizens of other than
German birth. Fathers of families got into the habit
every Christmas of going out into the forests surrounding New York to cut a young spruce or fir

tree for the holiday times. Or if they were rich enough to employ men-servants, they sent out the footman or the butler for this purpose.

It is said that a woodsman named Mark Carr, who was born among the foothills of the Catskill Mountains in the early part of the nineteenth century, was the first to make a regular business of Christmas trees. He had heard or read of the holiday festivities in the great city of New York, where churches and private parlors were hung with holly and hemlock leaves, and a pine or a fir tree stood in the middle of the nursery, covered with presents for the children.

It occurred to him that the young fir trees growing on the mountain-sides all around his little country home might be made use of for these holiday purposes. He could run no great risks in making trial of the idea. All he could lose was the time it took him to chop the trees down and bring them into market and the cost of a few days' living in New York.

In December, 1851, he put his plan into practice. Early in the month he and his boys loaded a couple of great sleds with young trees cut down from the neighboring forests, and having hitched a yoke of oxen to each sled drove them through the deep snow to the Hudson River at Catskill, whence the father started with them to the city.

One old-fashioned silver dollar secured the use of a strip of sidewalk on the corner of Greenwich and

Vesey streets. Here the hopeful mountaineer arranged his forest novelties for Christmas buyers. Nor had he long to wait. Customers flocked to his corner. Starting with moderate prices he soon raised them, as tree after tree left his hands, to sums that he would have deemed fabulous when he first dreamed of the experiment.

Next year he returned to the same place with a much larger stock, and "from that time to this," says Hexamer, an old historian of New York, "business has continued to exist until now hundreds of thousands of trees are yearly sold from Mark Carr's old corner."

At the present day, Christmas tree choppers usually begin work about the first of November. Thus they avoid the early snow falls which are liable greatly to increase the difficulties of the business by melting and freezing again on the trees and making their branches too brittle.

Firs and pines growing in open spaces are preferred to those in dense woodlands because they are more stocky and symmetrical. As the trees are felled the woodsmen pile them up beside the forest roads, where they will keep fresh and green for weeks or if necessary for months.

The balsam fir is the favorite for Christmas trees in the middle and eastern states. Its leaves retain their color and elasticity longer than those of the black spruce, of which large numbers are however shipped into markets further south.

CHAPTER XI

THE STORY OF THE THREE KINGS

In the Latin countries, that is to say, in Italy and the southernmost edge of France, Switzerland and Austria, our good old friend Santa Klaus rarely acts as the bearer of gifts at the Christmas season. Even Russia, though she has adopted Saint Nicholas as her patron saint, and celebrates his day in her own way, gives him no special place in the festivities that attend the birthday of Christ.

Indeed in all these countries it is not Christmas but the Epiphany, not December 25th but January 6th, which is the day on which presents are exchanged among friends and relations.

Epiphany, best known among English-speaking peoples as Twelfth Day, is the feast of the Three Kings, who figure in the New Testament story as the Magi or Wise Men of the East. You will undoubtedly remember how these Wise Men were warned of the birth of Christ by the appearance of a strange star in the heavens, and how, by following its guidance they arrived at the stable in Bethlehem where the Savior had been born.

On the way to Bethlehem.

Painting by J. Portaels.

They brought with them gifts of gold, frankincense and myrrh which they presented to the Holy
Child.

It was in memory of the gift-bearing kings that
Epiphany among the Latin and Russian peoples is
celebrated as the season for exchanging presents.

Little is said in the New Testament about these
wise men. Popular legend has greatly filled out the
Biblical story. It makes them three rich and powerful monarchs:—Caspar, King of Tarsus, the land of
myrrh; Melchior, King of Arabia, where the land is
ruddy with gold, and Balthasar, King of Saba, where
frankincense flows from the trees.

According to some authors these kings were of the
race of Balaam, the Old Testament prophet, who had
prepared the Gentiles for the coming of Christ into
the world. He had foretold that a new star should
appear in that part of the sky under which lay the
land of Judea, and had warned his descendants that
when they saw the star they should follow it and
should go to adore a great king who would be born
somewhere in Judea and be Lord of the Universe.

Even from the time of Balaam, it is added, senti-
nels had been posted upon a mountain towards the
east, in order that as soon as the star rose into view
they should give notice of it to the lords of the country, that the latter might go without delay to pay
reverence to the new king. This notice, as it hap-

pened, was not necessary in the case of Caspar, Melchior and Balthasar. Being very wise and learned kings they were under the special care of the Holy Spirit, who informed them in person of the appearance of the star.

Each of them at once gathered together a retinue of servants, as well as troops of horses, camels and dromedaries, all of which were laden with the choicest products of their respective countries. Then they started out in search of the new born king. They looked up to the star as their guide, for it moved forward as they moved, and they well knew that it had been sent to show them the way.

Where the three kings met is not told, but they arrived in Jerusalem together. As soon as they had entered the city gates the star which had guided them disappeared.

Now this was in accordance with the will of God,—that on the failure of their starry guide the kings might make inquiries in the capital of Judea, and by these means publish abroad the birth of the Son of God. Hence Herod and the Jews in general could have no excuse for ignoring this great event, and "the care and diligence of the Magi would reprove their negligence and indifference, because having Christ so near them, they did not seek Him, while these strangers came from distant countries for this cause alone."

The Three Kings visit Herod.
Painting by Sebastian Conca.

And in fact the three kings, as they rode through the streets of Jerusalem, asked of every one they met: "Where is He who is born King of the Jews? We have seen the star and have lost it."

None could give them any information, for no one in Jerusalem had seen the star.

One of the writers who tells this legend pauses to praise the "holy boldness" with which the Magi published a new king in Jerusalem without having fear of Herod who might have been capable of putting them to death for this cause. This writer quotes with approval the words which Saint John Chrysostom later addressed in imagination to the kings.

"Tell me, oh good kings, do you not know that whoever proclaims a new king in the life of a reigning king is liable to death, that you do this thing, and thus place yourselves in manifest danger from Herod, who may easily command you to be put to death?"

The same writer quotes with similar approval Saint John's answer to his own question:—

"The faith of these kings was so great and the love they bore to the new-born King so fervent, that even before they had seen Him they were ready to die for love of Him."[1]

The news of how three great kings, with a vast following of servants and beasts of burden had ar-

[1] "Il Libro D'oro. Translated by Mrs. Frances Alexander," Boston, Little Brown & Co. 1905.

rived in Jerusalem soon reached the ears of King Herod. He was greatly troubled when he heard that they had come in quest of a new-born King of the Jews, well knowing that the kingdom of Judea did not belong to him by succession or by birth, but that he had received it as a reward from the Romans, who had unjustly taken possession of it.

The first thing he did was to call together all the wise and learned men of Jerusalem, and ask them what the prophets had said about the coming of the Messiah, and the place where he would make his first appearance on earth.

And when they answered that the babe would be born in Bethlehem he was still more troubled. He at once sent out messengers to invite the kings to his palace, where he prepared a great banquet for them. After they had feasted he advised them to continue their journey as far as the little town of Bethlehem, where they might come upon the object of their quest.

"If you find that the child of prophecy has been born there," he added, "hasten back and tell me the joyful news that I, too, may come and worship Him."

The kings promised to do as Herod bid them, little knowing the guile and deceit that festered in his wicked heart. Then they resumed their journey.

No sooner had they issued out of the gate of Jerusalem than the star once more appeared in the sky, to their great joy. Following it, they arrived at the

The Journey of the Three Kings.
Painting by Andrea del Sarto.

house where, thirteen days before, Christ had been born.

Here the star stood still, burning even more brightly than ever, as if to say,

"Here is He whom you seek; this is the palace of the new-born King; this is the court of heaven, since here its King has His abode."

Strange and complex must have been the emotions these wise men felt in their hearts when they saw what the star showed them—this chamber of the King whom they sought, a place more suitable for beasts than for men; since not for men but for beasts had it been prepared.

Within the stable the virgin mother was watching over the manger, wherein lay her Divine Son.   Her quick ear caught the sound of footsteps and hoof-beats outside the door.   In great alarm she lifted the Child out of the manger and encircled Him with her arms.   This was the attitude in which the three kings, entering, found the mother and the Child.

The scales fell from their eyes at the sight.   They now realized that it was in truth no human king who had been born into the world, but the King of Heaven who had taken upon himself a human form.   Throwing themselves upon their knees, one by one they approached him, and worshipped him as God and the Savior of man.

Then they presented Him with their gifts which

had now acquired a new meaning. Caspar's gold testified that the babe was a king, Melchior's frankincense showed that he was God, and Balthasar's myrrh was a reminder that he was a man and doomed to suffer a painful death.

For gold was kept in kings' treasuries, frankincense was burnt in divine worship, and myrrh was used in embalming the bodies of the dead.

The infant Jesus returned their offerings with gifts more precious still. For gold He gave charity and spiritual riches, for incense, faith, for myrrh, truth and meekness.

That night the kings were warned in a dream that they should not go back by way of Jerusalem because King Herod cherished evil designs against the child Jesus, but that they should return by other roads to their own kingdoms. They obeyed in all meekness and humility.

"From this arose the custom," says the quaint old author I have already quoted, "which the church observes in processions, of leaving the church by one road and returning to it by another. By this it would be well that all Christians should learn from the Magi not only to see Christ, but having found Him again, even though they had lost Him, to return by a different way from the other; because if at first they walked in the ways of sin, they should return to it

The Arrival of the Three Kings.
Painting by Bernardo Luini.

by the ways of holiness; and in this country they will
arrive at the true country, which is heaven."

When Herod found that the three kings had returned home without fulfilling their promise to him he
was greatly wroth. It was then that he issued his edict
commanding that all children under the age of two
years should be put to death. He hoped that the
Messiah would be slaughtered among the rest. But,
as the New Testament tells us, the Holy Family received a special warning from heaven and fled into
Egypt before the emissaries of wicked King Herod
could reach them.

As to the three kings, when they had arrived, each
at his own capital, they cast aside their royal robes and
abandoned their royal state. Giving all their goods
to the poor they wandered about the earth annnounc-
ing that the Savior of man had been born in Bethlehem.

Seven years after the death of Christ upon the
cross the wise men were found in India by Saint
Thomas, once the doubting disciple, now become firm
in the faith, and an apostle to the East. Saint
Thomas baptized them in the name of the Father
and the Son and the Holy Ghost, and they too became
missionaries of the gospel. In the end they fell mar-
tyrs for their faith and their bodies were all buried
together outside the walls of Jerusalem.

Three hundred years passed away. Then Saint Helena, mother of the Emperor Constantine, made her famous pilgrimage to Palestine. Though she was quite eighty years of age she was still full of life and vigor. All her time and energies she devoted to the discovery of early Christian remains. She is credited with the finding of the cross on which Christ suffered and the tomb in which He was buried.

She also identified the tomb of the Three Kings and carried their bodies away with her, on her return journey to Constantinople, to re-bury them in the church of Saint Sophia. Later the remains were transferred to Milan and later still to Cologne. There they are still shown, in a side chapel of the great Cathedral, lying in a golden shrine—their grinning skulls girt with golden crowns, and their skeleton bodies clad in royal purple, bedecked with jewels of enormous value.

This is the story of the Three Kings as it is related all over Europe. In the Latin countries and in Russia, an episode is added which is unknown in other lands.

On their way from Jerusalem to Bethlehem, so this added legend runs, the three kings came across an old woman who was cleaning up her house.

She asked them whither they were going. And when they told her that they were on their way to

The Adoration of the Magi.
Painting by Fra Angelico.

pay homage to the new-born King of the Jews she prayed them to tarry until she had finished her task.

"Fain would I go with you," she pleaded, "and join in your homage."

"Nay," replied the kings, "we have no time to wait. But leave your work and come with us."

The old woman refused to leave her work until it was all finished. Then it was too late. She strove, indeed, to follow the kings, but they were lost to sight.

Ever since that day she has been wandering about the earth seeking for the child Jesus. And on the eve of the Epiphany she comes down the chimneys of the houses, leaving gifts for the little ones, as the kings left gifts for the infant Jesus, and hoping against hope that she may find Him whom she still seeks.

In Italy she is known to this day as the Befana (a corruption of Epiphania, the Italian for Epiphany) and in Russia as the Baboushka or little old woman.

On the eve of Epiphany, Italian children hang up their clothes, after carefully emptying the pockets, around the huge fireplaces which are common both in palaces and in hovels. During the night the Befana comes down the chimney, just like Santa Klaus on Christmas eve. If the children have been good, she stuffs their pockets full of candies and other presents, but if they have been bad all they get from her are charcoal ashes or birchrods.

In Spain, however, it is not the Befana nor the Baboushka, but one of the three kings, no less a person indeed than Balthazar, who is the gift bearer. On the eve of the Epiphany children leave their shoes and boots out in some convenient spot near the chimney, expecting Balthazar will fill them during the night.

From early times he has been represented as a blackamoor or negro. But not from the earliest. In the pictures by Giotto and Fra Angelico representing the Adoration of the Magi, Balthazar is shown as a white man. In a picture on the same subject by Bernardo Luini he appears with the woolly hair, black face and thick lips of the negro.

Somewhere between the time of Fra Angelico and Bernardo Luini, Balthazar changed his skin and became a colored gentleman.

In many Italian cities, it is the custom of shopkeepers to decorate their windows with puppets meant to represent the three kings. Conspicuous among these grins the black face of Balthazar.

There is a poem by the famous Dean Trench which was probably suggested by Luini's picture. Here are some of the most striking lines. They will show you how closely the poem follows the picture:

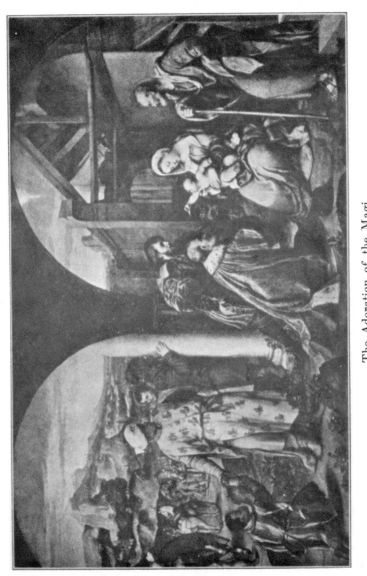

The Adoration of the Magi.
Painting by Veronese.

From what region of the morn
Are ye come, thus travel-worn,
With those boxes pearl-embost,
Caskets rare, and gifts of cost?
While your swarth attendants wait
At the stable's outer gate,
And the camels lift their head
High above the lowly shed;
Or are seen, a long-drawn train,
Winding down into the plain,
From below the light-blue line
Of the hills in distance fine,
Dear for your own sake, whence are ye?
Dearer for the mystery
That is round you—on what skies
Gazing, saw you first arise,
Thro' the darkness, that clear star,
Which has marshall'd you so far,
Even unto this strawy tent,
Dancing up the Orient?
Shall we name you Kings indeed,
Or is this our idle creed?
Kings of Seba, with the gold
And the incense long foretold?
Would the Gentile world by you
First-fruits pay of tribute due;
Or have Israel's scatter'd race,
From their unknown hiding-place,
Sent to claim their part and right
In the Child new-born to-night?

An older poet than Trench, the seventeenth century George Wither, has woven some pretty fancies
about the story of the wise men as it is told by Saint
Matthew in the New Testament.

That so thy blessed birth, oh Christ,
   Might through the world be spread about,
Thy Starre appeared in the East,
   Whereby the Gentiles found thee out;
And, off'ring Thee Myrrh, Incense, Gold,
Thy threefold Office did unfold.

Sweet Jesus, let that Starre of Thine,
   Thy Grace, which guides to find out Thee,
Within our hearts for ever shine,
   That Thou of us found out maist bee:
And Thou shalt be our King, therefore,
Our Priest, and Prophet evermore.

Teares that from true repentance drop,
   Instead of Myrrhe, present will wee:
For Incense, we will offer up
   Our Praiers and Praises unto Thee;
And bring for Gold each pious deed,
Which doth from saving faith proceed.

And as those Wise men never went
   To visit Herod any more;
So, finding Thee, we will repent
   Our courses follow'd heretofore:
And that we homeward may retire,
Our way by Thee we will enquire.

The Adoration of the Three Kings.

From the painting by E. Burne Jones.

CHAPTER XII

SOME TWELFTH NIGHT CUSTOMS

As Twelfth Night, or Epiphany, is a day dedicated to the three Wise Men of the New Testament—the three kings of popular legend—it is only natural that one or more kings should be everywhere prominent in the celebration of the holiday.

The full trio are present in many places. Thus in Milan, Italy, three young men dress themselves up in royal robes on Epiphany morning and mounting horses as splendidly attired as themselves appear before the city gates. They are admitted with loud cheers, and a procession is formed. Before the kings marches a man bearing a large gilt star; behind them the citizens fall into line. At every street corner new batches of citizens join the parade. They file through the streets to the cathedral. At its steps the kings dismount, and, with their followers, march up the aisle to the high altar where a figure of the infant Christ lies in a manger. Every one who wishes may leave a present in the manger. Then the procession disbands.

In Madrid a bit of practical joking is still indulged

in on Epiphany eve. The peasants from miles around flock into the city at that time. Many of them are very ignorant and very superstitious. The town folk think it funny to gather together in small crowds all playing on noisy horns and thumping discordant drums. The mobs parade up and down the streets. Their great delight is to fall in with some simpleton who is new to city ways. Such a man is easily made to believe that they are on their way to meet the three kings, who are expected to arrive at one of the gates some time that night.

The mob urge the countryman to join them. If he consents they throw over his neck a mule collar with a string of bells attached to it. Then a step ladder is thrust into his hands. To the jingling of his own bells the poor yokel is made to carry the ladder through the streets. At every one of the gates of the city the mob halt and command their victim to climb up the ladder and peer over the walls to see if the kings are anywhere in sight.

Sometimes when he reaches the top the poor wretch is allowed to fall, at the risk of a cracked head or a broken limb. If he escapes all dangers, he is led on from gate to gate until his patience or his faith is exhausted.

In England, as well as in France, a single king survives in the ceremony of the Twelfth Cake.

The Child's Twelfth Night Dream.

Drawing by John Leech.

France, which was probably the inventor of this eatable, known there as the King's Cake, cherishes the custom with especial gusto. So let us begin with the Galette du Roi.

The size of the cake is determined by the number of the guests for whom it is to be served. It is usually made of pastry and is baked in a round sheet like a pie. A broad bean was formerly baked into the cake, but in our day a wee little china image is usually substituted for the bean. When ready the cake is cut into slices and the youngest child at the table directs how these slices shall be distributed to the others. There is great excitement as slice after slice is handed out and eaten.

At last some one's teeth come in contact with the image and he spits it out. "He," I say, on the supposition that it is a boy. If it is, indeed, a boy, he is called King of the Bean (le Roi Favette), and chooses a queen from among the girls. If it be a girl she becomes queen and chooses a boy as her consort.

King and queen are now closely watched by their companions. When either of them drinks the whole party has to cry out "The king drinks" or "the queen drinks," as the case may be. Any one who fails to join in the cry has to pay a forfeit.

In England the custom varies in different localities as it has varied at different dates.

What it was in London during the middle of the nineteenth century is best described by Hone in his "Table Book:"

"First buy your cake," says this author. "Next, look at your invitation list, and count the number of ladies you expect, and afterwards the number of gentlemen.

"Then you write down on slips of paper the names of as many famous characters in history, male and female, as will cover the list of guests. Add to each slip some pleasant bit of verse.

"Fold them up exactly of the same size, and number each on the back; taking care to make the king No. 1 and the queen No. 2. Cause tea and coffee to be handed to your visitors as they drop in. When all are assembled and tea is over, put as many ladies' characters in a reticule as there are ladies present; next put the gentlemen's characters in a hat. Then call on a gentleman to carry the reticule to the ladies as they sit; from which each lady is to draw one ticket and to preserve it unopened. Select a lady to bear the hat to the gentlemen, for the same purpose. There will be one ticket left in the reticule, and another in the hat,—which the lady and gentleman who carried each is to interchange, as having fallen to each. Next arrange your visitors, according to their numbers; —the king No. 1, the queen No. 2 and so on. The king is then to recite the verse on his ticket; then the queen a verse on hers; and so the characters are to proceed in numerical order.

"This done, let the cake and refreshments go round; and hey! for merriment!"

In earlier days, however, we know that the cake played a more important part in the festivities than Hone allows to it.   In fact the English here closely followed the French fashion which I have already described, although in England the King's bean was supplemented by a pea for the Queen.   This much we may learn from a poem by Robert Herrick, who lived in the seventeenth century:

> Now, now, the mirth comes
> With the cake full of plums,
> Where bean is the king of the sport here;
> Beside we must know,
> The pea also
> Must revel as queen in the court here.

> Begin then to choose
> This night as ye use,
> Who shall for the present delight here;
> Be a king by the lot,
> And who shall not
> Be Twelfth-day Queen for the night here.

CHAPTER XIII

ST. NICHOLAS is practically forgotten to-day in Protestant England. But in the merrie England of olden times, before the Catholic religion had given way to Protestantism, he was one of the most popular saints in the calendar.

This is shown not only by the number of churches dedicated in his honor, but also by the number of boys who received his name in baptism. Nicholases were once as common among the Englishmen of the past as Maries were among English women. A curious fact may be brough up in evidence. In English catechisms, whose forms date from a very early time, the question is put to the pupil:

"What is your name?"

And the answer is printed thus: "N. or M." Of course the pupil is expected to put his or her name in place of these initials. Now it is probable that N stands for Nicholas and M for Mary, and the choice of these initials was made not only because Nicholas was the patron of boys and Mary of girls, but because these were the commonest names in Old England.

The feast of St. Nicholas used to be celebrated by a ceremony known as the election of a Boy-bishop. This custom existed to some extent on the continent of Europe, but it nowhere flourished so vigorously as in England. It has been traced as far back as the thirteenth century.

To the choir boys and altar boys of English churches it was a particularly exciting time.

On St. Nicholas' eve all the boys who sang in the choir or served at the altar met at their parish church, or in the great cathedral, if they belonged to a bishop's see, and elected one from among their number, who took the title of "the Boy-bishop." This title with its dignities he retained until December 28th, Holy Innocents' Day, so called because it is the anniversary of the slaughter of the children in Palestine by order of the wicked King Herod.

The Boy-bishop was dressed in the robes of a real bishop. On his head was placed a mitre, in his right hand a crozier. Another boy was elected dean, while the rest were styled canons, all being dressed in the robes of their office.

During the three weeks from December 5 to December 28, the Boy-bishop could perform all the duties of a real bishop, except that of saying mass. If a priest died during the period when he held office he could appoint another to take his place in the church left vacant. If he himself died before Holy

Innocents' Day he was given a bishop's grand funeral in the cathedral.

"There is a little tomb of this kind," says Miss Abbie Farwell Brown, "not half the size of a full-grown one, in a great cathedral that I know. It is of white marble, grandly carved and decorated, and though it is worn and nicked by eight hundred years of change, one can plainly see that it is a child's face among the long curls beneath the bishop's mitre. No one knows his name, nor aught about him, save that he must be one of the Boy-bishops who died at Christmas time, or he would not be buried in the great cathedral tomb." [1]

Doubtless Miss Brown has in mind the cathedral of Salisbury, England. In the nave of that great minster there is just such a tomb, with just such a likeness carved upon it. The boy's foot rests on the figure of a monster with a lion's head and a dragon's tail, in allusion to the words of the psalmist "Thou shalt tread on the lion and the dragon."

But to continue. On December 6th the newly elected Boy-bishop with his dean and canons held a grand service in the church to which they were attached, the prayers being chanted in the boy's sweet childish voice. A great crowd always thronged the church to gaze on so rare a sight, and the offerings that they made were all for the Boy-bishop.

[1] Lippincott's Magazine.

After the services were over the bishop and his boy-assistants would form themselves into a procession and parade through the streets of the town or the lanes of the countryside, asking some small money tributes from all they met and at every door where they knocked. This was known as the Bishop's Subsidy and though no one was likely to give a great deal, yet as the procession was continued every day during the three weeks, the amount collected sometimes rolled up into quite a pretty sum.

Faster and more furious grew the fun as the time of the bishop's rule neared its close. On the afternoon of December 27th little Nicholas and his companions sang vespers, while the real priests of the church acted as altar boys and choristers. Then the Boy-bishop gave a solemn benediction to all present. Making the sign of the cross over the kneeling throngs, he dismissed them with the words:

Crucis signo vos consigno; vestra sit tuitio,
Quos nos emit et redemit suae carnis pretio.

These latin words being translated into English mean:
"I bestow upon you the sign of the cross, yours be it to learn what is sent for our redemption through the price of his flesh."

Next day (the actual feast of the Holy Innocents), the Boy-bishop preached a sermon which usually was written for him by some famous prelate. On his dismissal of the congregation at the close of the sermon, the festival of the Boy-bishop was at an end.

When Henry VIII became a Protestant and brought over a great many of his subjects to the new faith one of his first acts was to abolish the Boy-bishop and his festival. Henry's daughter, Queen Mary, restored both for the few years of her own reign, but Queen Elizabeth, her sister and successor, put an end to the mummery forever.

We catch our last glimpse of the Boy-bishop in the pages of a historian called William Strype, who informs us that on the fifth day of December, 1556, (Queen Mary being then still alive) "a boy habited like a bishop in pontificalibus, went abroad in most parts of London, singing after the old fashion, and was received by many ignorant but well disposed people into their houses, and had as much good cheer as was ever wont to be had before, at least in many places."

Old customs die hard. We have come across many instances of the truth of this saying in the course of our study of the Christmas festivals. Just as Christianity had to retain and remodel many old heathen customs, so Protestantism (often without meaning it) retained and remodeled many an old Catholic custom. Just as Silenus, and Saturn, survived in a measure as Santa Claus, so the Boy-bishop, in a measure, survived as the hero of a ceremony which flourished at the school of Eton until nearly the middle of the nineteenth century.

This was known as Eton Montem. It was celebrated not in December but in June, though tradition tells us that the original date was St. Nicholas Day and that the ceremony was instituted in the year 1440, the very year when Eton was founded.

Later it took place every third year on the Tuesday after Whitsunday or Pentecost, which usually falls in June. On that day a procession of all the scholars went from the school buildings to a hill known as Salt Hill that rises just outside of the grounds. At their head marched the captain and his chaplain, the one being the head boy of the highest class in school, the other the head boy of the second class. The chaplain was dressed in a suit of priestly black with a bushy wig upon his head.

Two boys called "salt bearers" with "scouts" dressed like old-time footmen ran beside the procession begging from all passersby and they scattered through the roads to beg at the doors of houses for miles around.

The money thus collected was put into a great bag, already sprinkled with a small quantity of salt and at the end of the day this bag was handed over to the captain. It was used to pay his expenses when he left Eton for some one of the great universities. Not infrequently it mounted up to hundreds of dollars and sometimes even to a thousand or more.

Up to the middle of the eighteenth century it was customary for the chaplain to read prayers on Salt Hill. He was assisted by a clerk whom he kicked down hill at their conclusion. The irreverence of this part of the ceremony shocked Queen Caroline and at her request it was ever afterwards omitted. In 1847 the entire ceremony was abolished by act of Parliament, the last celebration having taken place on June 28th, 1844.

And thus the last vestige of Saint Nicholas passed out of the ceremonial life of England.

CHAPTER XIV

FATHER CHRISTMAS AND HIS FAMILY

THE English, as I have said, have no Saint Nicholas, no Santa Klaus, no Chris-kinkle to act as a distributor of gifts on Christmas eve. They hail as the patron of the season a vague allegorical being, usually called Father Christmas, though he has, sometimes, been known also as Old Christmas, Captain Christmas, and by other titles.

He appears only in picture, in poetry, and in dramatic pieces specially got up for the holidays. In the latter he has played an important part from a very early period. The most famous of such pieces was a "masque" written by Ben Jonson, Shakespeare's friend and rival, and produced at the court of King James I in the year 1616. That, by the way, is the very year of Shakespeare's death.

Christmas festivities at that time were frowned down upon by many of the more zealous Protestants— just then beginning to earn the name of "Puritans"— who fancied that these mummeries and rejoicings smacked too strongly of "Papist" or Roman Catholice tendencies. Indeed many fanatics had striven to abolish Christmas altogether, and had partly succeeded in doing so, at least among the people who believed as they did. But James I, though a foolish person in some respects was a learned man and a great lover of the traditions of the past.

It is in allusion to the Puritan attempt to suppress him altogether that Ben Jonson's Father Christmas utters these words as he makes his entrance upon the stage:

"Why, gentlemen, do you know what you do? Ha! would you have kept me out? CHRISTMAS!—Old Christmas—Christmas of London, and Captain Christmas! Pray you let me be brought before my Lord Chamberlain; I'll not be answered else. ' *'Tis merry in hall, when beards wag all.*' I have seen the time you have wished for me, for a merry Christmas, and now you have me, they would not let me in: *I must come another time!* A good jest—as if I could come more than once a year. Why, I am no dangerous person, and so I told my friends of the guard. I am old Gregory Christmas, still, and, though I come out of the Pope's Head-alley, as good a Protestant as any in my parish."

He must have been a quaint looking figure, this same Father Christmas, for we are told that his costume consisted of

"round hose, long stockings, close doublet, high-crowned hat, with a brooch, long, thin beard, truncheon, little ruffs,

Father Christmas.

Drawn by Kenny Meadows.
From the Illustrated London News, December, 1847.

white shoes, with his scarfs and garters tied cross, and his drum beaten before him,"

And now, to the sound of the drum, in troop all his merry family—sons and daughters and nephews and nieces.   Among them are the Lord of Misrule, who in old days directed the Christmas revels; Roast Beef, "that English Champion bold," who has saved many a sturdy Englishman from starvation; Plum Pudding, a blackamoor, with rich round face and rosemary cockade; and Minced Pie, and Baby Cake, and Mumming and Wassail and Offering and Carol, and New Year's Gift, and others too numerous to mention.

Many members of this robust family will be recognized as contributors to the Christmas cheer of to-day.   Others have disappeared forever.

The Lord of Misrule, for example, the "Grand Captain of Mischief," as the Puritans called him, no longer summons around him all the madcap youths of town or village for a brief period of lawless revelry.

In Scotland this personage was known as the Abbot of Unreason, a name which clearly shows that he was a direct descendant from the chief performer in the mediæval Feast of Fools, and as such was a great-great-etc.-grandson of Silenus, the merrymaker in the Greek Bacchanalia.

King James I of England was succeeded by his
son Charles I. During the reign of the latter un-
happy monarch, the Puritan party in England gathered so much strength that, under the lead of Oliver
Cromwell, they hurled Charles from his throne and
cut off his head, sending his entire family into exile
for a period of a dozen years. Father Christmas
shared the exile of his royal patrons, or if he dared
show his face in England at all, it was only here and
there in remote country places or behind locked doors
in the obscurer parts of the great cities. Meanwhile
his absence was greatly deplored by that part of the
English people who had remained loyal to the crown.
One of these put forward a curious little book entitled "An Hue and Cry after Christmas." The following paragraph shows the spirit in which the book
was written:

"Any man or woman, that can give any knowledge,
or tell any tidings of an old, old, very old grey-
bearded gentleman, called Christmas, who was wont
to be a very familiar guest and visit all sorts of people, both poor and rich, and used to appear in glit-
tering gold, silk and silver, in the court, and in all
shapes in the theatre in White Hall, and had ringing, feasts and jollity in all places, both in the city
and the country, for his coming—whoever can tell
what is become of him, or where he may be found, let
him bring him back again into England."

Father Christmas, another conception.

Drawing by Kenny Meadows.

Well, Father Christmas did come back to England in the train of Charles I's son, Charles II who shortly after Cromwell's death was restored to the English throne by the wish of the majority of the English people.

When he resumed the rule that had been wrested by the Puritans from his father the old celebrations of Christmas were to some extent revived in the royal and other mansions and at the theatres.

"To some extent"—that is too often a sad phrase!

It means, in this case, that pretty much all the life and spirit of the old ceremonies had departed so that no revival could restore them to their former vitality.

The changes wrought by the troublous times through which England had passed were fatal to the old-time splendors of the Christmas season. In the country many of the great old estates had passed into new hands and the old ties between the lord of the manor and his tenants had been forever sundered. The rafters of the old baronial halls no longer rang with the merriment which had graced the meeting of master and servants on a holiday basis of equality. Friends and relatives who from childhood had gathered together around the Yule log were now scattered or had been slain by the chances of war. Members of old country families deprived by Cromwell of their estates and driven into exile, now flocked to London to become hangers-on at the court of a "Merry Monarch" whose mirth was often bought at the expense of his subject's years.

The Merry Monarch, himself (that was the name given to Charles II), was a prodigal and a spendthrift, who found all sorts of new ways in which to squander the money raised by taxes from his subjects. He had little left, therefore, to imitate the splendid pageants that distinguished the courts of Queen Elizabeth and James I at the ancient holiday seasons.

A famous song called "The Old and Young Courtier" was written shortly after Charles II had regained his throne. It sadly contrasts the good old times and the good old people with the bad new times and the bad new people of the Restoration.

The old courtier is lovingly described as "a worshipful old gentleman who had a great estate," with a lovely old wife by his side, and a great band of servants around them. Then followed this verse:

With a good old fashion when Christmas was come,
To call in all his old neighbors with bagpipe and drum,
With good cheer enough to furnish every room,
And old liquor able to make a cat speak, and man dumb;
   Like an old courtier of the queen's
   And the queen's old courtier.

'A contrast is drawn between this old courtier of the

The Old and the New Christmas.
From London Punch, Dec. 24, 1881.

queen's and the young courtier of the king's, with all
his new fangled notions, and especially

With a new fashion, when Christmas is drawing on,
On a new journey to London we must straight all begone
And leave none to keep house but our new porter John
Who relieves the poor with a thump in the back with a stone.
      Like a young courtier of the king's
      And the king's young courtier.

From time to time, even in periods nearer to our
own, complaints have been raised in England that
the spirit of the old-time Christmas merriment has
departed forever, and that good old Father Christmas is once more an exile from his own.

A cartoon by Linley M. Sambourne published in
the *London Punch* for December 24, 1881, shows the
Old-Fashioned Christmas holding a lively conversa-
tion with the New.

This prose bit is printed beneath the picture:

Christmas (*New Style*). "WE ARE THE MODERN CHRIST-
MAS CARDS—WE ARE! WE ARE! WE ARE!"

Christmas (*Old Style*). "YOU REPRESENT CHRISTMAS!
POOH! WHAT DO YOU MEAN BY COMING OUT LIKE THAT AT
THIS TIME OF YEAR?"

Then follows this poem, which still further explains
the meaning of the picture:

Says the Old-fashioned Christmas to the New-fangled Christ-
    mas,
  " 'Pon my word, my boy, I don't think much of you."
Says the New-fangled Christmas to the Old-fashioned Christ-
    mas,
  "Well, with tastes like yours, I don't suppose you do.
For, to celebrate a season, very fortunately brief,
At *your* age too,—with an orgie of plum-pudding and roast
    beef,
Crowned with holly, in a dressing-gown!   The thing 's past
    all belief !"
  Says Old Christmas, with a nod, "My boy, that 's true."

Says the New-fangled Christmas to the Old-fashioned Christ-
    mas,
  "For tomfoolery like yours we have no zest."
Says the Old-fashioned Christmas to the New-fangled Christ-
    mas,
  "What now !   *You* to talk like that !   Well, I am blest !
'Tomfoolery'?   Why, what do you call all this here modern
    fad,—
Sending gimcrack cards by dozens, dauby, glaring, good, and
    bad,
Nymphs—and what not?   Why, between you, you drive
    friends and Postmen mad."
  Says Young Christmas, "When it 's over, they can rest."

Says the Old-fashioned Christmas to the New-fangled Christ-
    mas,
  "Where 's the jollity of twenty years ago?"

Bringing in Old Christmas.

From the Illustrated London News.

Says the New-fangled Christmas to the Old-fashioned Christ-
    mas,
  "How on earth, now, do you think that *I* should know?
For to-day, with Art and Culture's dainty trifles by the score,
We just manage to scrape through the time, confessing it 's
    a bore;
But, by Jove, if *you* came back again, 'twould soon be some-
    thing more!"
  Says Old Christmas, "Well, I really call that low."

Says the New-fangled Christmas to the Old-fashioned Christ-
    mas,
  "I don't see the day a bit, you know, like you."
Says the Old-fashioned Christmas to the New-fangled Christ-
    mas,
  "Never mind, my boy, there 's something you can do.
Have your fads; but copy me, my boy. Go on as I 've be-
    gun.
Remember, when your table 's spread, the thousands that have
    none.
So, get your cheque-book out, my boy. Show you 're your
    father's son."
  Says Young Christmas, "Well, I don't mind if I do."

After all, may it not be safe for us to decide that
it is not the spirit but the fashion which alters, that
the heart of Old Father Christmas still beats warm
under the new garb wherein changing tastes have
clothed him? Surely, if we have dropped some of
the revellings of the past, we have dropped also the

abuses which gradually made distasteful the horse play that attended those revelries.

On the whole the "new fangled Christmas" has many points that show an improvement over the old-fashioned Christmas while in all essentials the two remain one and the same.

Some humble members of Father Christmas' family still surviving to a small extent in London are the "waits" or wandering musicians who play dismal tunes under the windows of the well-to-do in the hopes of obtaining a few pennies.

These are direct descendants from the "jongleurs" or minstrels who in the Middle Ages celebrated the birth of Christ on Christmas night with song and dance.

The Christmas Waits.

Drawing by Kenny Meadows.
From the Illustrated London News, December, 1848.

CHAPTER XV

SOME people still living (but they must be very aged people by now) may be able to remember the pantomime which was one of the great features of the Christmas holidays in early nineteenth century England, and may be looked upon as the legitimate successor of the ancient "masque." The word pantomime comes from two Greek words meaning "all mimicry." It is a play in which the actors say never a word but perform their parts in dumb show, that is, by signs and gestures. Being almost unknown in America this word of explanation may be necessary.

England borrowed the pantomime from Italy, where it has survived from the the masked frolics of the Roman Saturnalia. Pantaloon, Harlequin and the Fairy Columbine were the principal actors in all the Italian pantomimes and all of them wore masks.

A famous player named Rich, who was known on the stage as Lun, was the first to introduce pantomime into England. In the year 1717 he produced a play of this sort called Harlequin Executed, in which he himself performed the part of Harlequin. It is said that he "could describe to the audience by his signs and gestures as intelligibly as others could express by words." [1]

David Garrick, perhaps the greatest of all English actors, was a younger contemporary of Rich and after his friend's death he celebrated the silent but powerful language of Rich in these lines:

> When Lun appeared, with matchless grace and ishm,
> He gave the power of speech to every limb,
> Though masked and mute, conveyed his quick intent,
> And told in frolic gestures all he meant;
> But now the motley coat and sword of wood
> Require a tongue to make them understood.

By the last lines Garrick evidently means to say that spoken words had in his time been introduced into the so-called pantomime, because no actor remained who was capable of conveying his meaning by nod or wink or gesture in the old-time manner.

By the beginning of the nineteenth century, however, all and more of the original glories of pantomime were brought back to the English stage by Joseph Grimaldi, an Italian by birth, but an Englishman by adoption. He was the greatest clown known to the history of English drama.

[1] D'Israeli's "Curiosities of Literature."

Jongleurs announcing the birth of our Lord.

From a painting by A. F. Gorguet.

After his retirement, in 1828, pantomime still flourished for a number of years as the chief dramatic feature of the Christmas season.

St. Stephen's Day (December 26, the day after Christmas) was the day specially set aside for the production of a pantomime, but in due time those performances were extended all over the Christmas season. They were the particular delight of the young folk, though older folk also liked to attend them and live their youth over again in the joy reflected from the faces of the boys and girls in the audience.

Leigh Hunt, a charming English writer who never lost his boy-heart tells us how much pleasure he found in watching the children at a pantomime.

"I am more delighted," he says, "in watching the vivacious workings of their ingenuous countenances at these Christmas shows than at the sights themselves. . . . Stretching half over the boxes at the theatre, adorned by maternal love, see their enraptured faces, now turned to the galleries, wondering at their height and at the number of regular-placed heads contained in them; now directed towards the green cloud which is so lingeringly kept between them and their promised bliss. The half-peeled orange laid aside when the play begins; their anxiety for that which they understand; their honest laughter which runs through the house like a merry peal of sweet bells; the fear of the little girl lest they should discover the person hid behind the screen; the exultation of the boy when the hero conquers. But, oh, the rapture when the pantomime commences! Ready to leap out of the box, they joy in the mischief of the clown, laugh at the thwacks he gets for his meddling, and feel no small portion of contempt for his ignorance in not knowing that hot water will scald and gunpowder explode; while, with head aside to give fresh energy to the strokes, they ring their little palms against each other in testimony of exuberant delight."

Pantomime in the England of to-day has dwindled into a mere side show for spectacular ballets, which are now all the fashion. Clown and Columbine are indeed, occasionally introduced into these ballets but the clown is no longer a leading character and Columbine and her companions are selected more for their skill in dancing than in the art of gesture.

Very rarely, indeed, is a comic mask introduced into a Christmas piece nowadays. Formerly, Harlequin and Columbine wore little black masks that just covered the upper part of the face, while the rest of the jolly crew of elves, ogres and buffoons were disguised in huge headpieces arranged over their shoulders.

And here comes in the point of the picture by Mr. Potter which I have reproduced from the Christmas

Going to the Pantomime.

Drawing by John Leech.
From the Illustrated London News, December 24, 1853.

number of an English weekly called *The Sporting Times.*

The young woman of this picture is a "high-kick-er" who evidently has made a hit with the audience at a modern Christmas ballet. When she gets behind the scenes among "properties" left over from the ancient days, she gives a frisky vent to her feelings by flashing her heels in the faces of the grinning old masks.

In short, she represents pantomime in its most modern development, the ballet, as contrasted with the grotesque humors of the past.

You may find food for both humor and pathos, in the idea which Mr. Potter has worked out in this pretty and ingenious manner.

CHAPTER XVI

SAINT NICHOLAS IN EUROPE

THERE is no country in Europe where Saint Nicholas is more honored than in Holland. Even before his festival arrives—during all the first five days of December—the shops in town and city put on their most festive array. All the people in shop and street assume a brisk and bustling air. Dutch men and Dutch women, usually silent and stolid, hail one another with noisy greetings as they meet. Everybody, in short, has his best foot foremost.

Amsterdam, one of many cities which claim Saint Nicholas as their patron saint, is especially wideawake. During the first week of December the confectioners' shops are ablaze with all sorts of splendors in cake and candy. Sugar rabbits, sugar cats and sugar mice disport themselves amid scenery of sugar and chocolate and wood shavings. The shavings (painted a vivid green), supply the foliage for chocolate trees and candied fruits. In all shapes and sizes are figures of men and women made out of crisp brown gingerbread, called Saint Nicholas cake, which is specially prepared for the holiday. These figures are

194

Mute admiration.

By Raymond Potter.

sometimes known as "sweethearts" and it is a merry jest to send a girl figure to a boy and a boy figure to a girl. Nay the elders themselves are not forgotten if they are unmarried. It is good fun, we are told, to have a servant burst into a roomful of people and say to the lady of the house:

"If you please ma'am, here is Miss Annie's sweetheart," and hand over to mamma a gingerbread man for her little girl.[1]

Other jokes of the same kind are played with so-called "hearts," large and luscious pieces of marchpane moulded into the familiar shape supposed to resemble the organ that is supposed to be the seat of human affection. These are exchanged among the young people much as valentines, with us, are exchanged on February 14th.

"Of course," says the authority I have already quoted, a lady of Holland birth who speaks of what she herself has seen and experienced, "most girls like having such an innocent heart sent to them, and it is funny to see the mysterious look with which one tells another:

" 'I had a large heart sent to me last night. I cannot possibly think who sent it.' "

Here and there in the streets you will see groups of boys and girls clustered around a linen-draper's shop. For it is the linen drapers who especially love

[1] Annie C. Kuiper in "St. Nicholas" Magazine, January, 1897.

to display in their windows a life-like image of Saint Nicholas, ruddy faced, white bearded, crowned with his mitre and clad in his bright red robe lined with soft white fur, bearing a crozier in his hand, and mounted on a fiery white horse. Behind him stands his negro servant Jan, or John.

On December 5th, the eve of the saint's feast, he is said to ride over the roofs of the houses, dropping candies into the wide chimneys. And indeed, in houses where children believe this, their faith is rewarded by the fact that candies and other goodies do stream down into the great open hearths and are gathered in by eager little people who have been singing the saint's praises all through the evening.

In many households, moreover, the saint actually presents himself to the eyes of his worshippers and admirers. A knock is heard at the door; it is opened, and amid the breathless silence of the children, Santa Klaus, in flesh and blood, and in all the glory of scarlet robe and bejewelled mitre, steps into the room. He is closely followed by his servant Jan, who bears a basket containing all sorts of presents for the good children, and all sorts of unpleasant reminders for the bad ones.

Before these things are distributed, Santa Klaus calls up the children one by one. He praises the good ones for all the kind deeds they have done during the past year, while gently reproving any faults

Santa Claus comes to grief on an automobile.

Copyright 1908 by Life Publishing Company.

which may have mingled with their virtues. To the bad ones he is stern but just. He reminds them of their misdeeds, and tells them that he cannot give them any presents until they improve. If they have been very, very bad, he hands a birch rod over to their parents with the advice that it should be used upon their little backs in the task of reformation.

Great is the wonder that Santa Klaus should know so much about the children in a whole neighborhood. He goes, or is supposed to go, from house to house in the course of the day, and everywhere he praises the virtues or condemns the faults of the boys and girls arrayed to meet him. Sometimes it is found, by comparing notes, that he was in two or more houses at the same time.

Of course, you who have had your eyes opened, guess that the part of Santa Klaus is taken by some older member of each family, who confines his visits to his own circle of relatives. Except in very small villages, there are many Santa Klauses, therefore, going the rounds on Saint Nicholas's day, each well acquainted in the houses he visits.

In Austria, also, and in many parts of Southern Germany, St. Nicholas Eve is made memorable in every nursery by a visit from the saint. A well grown boy with a quick and clever mind and some knowledge of church doctrine, is chosen to play the part of Santa Klaus. He is masked in long white vestments. A silk scarf is wound around his neck, a mitre crowns his head, a crozier is put in his hand. He is attended by two angels and a whole troop of devils.

The angels are dressed much like the choir-boys you have seen in Catholic and Episcopalian churches, save that they also wear silken scarfs around their necks. Each carries a basket.

The devils blacken their faces, put horns upon their heads and decorate their faces with pig's snouts or any other grotesque device that may suggest itself to their fancy. All are girt with chains, which they shake or rattle furiously.

Boy-like, it is thought much better fun to play devil than angel, and any boy who can lay his hands upon a suitable costume is at liberty to join the infernal train.

Late in the afternoon of December 5th the Boy-bishop and his attendants begin their round of visits. It is the season for young folks' parties, and all the children of the village who are not masquerading as bishop or angel or imp have gathered together in a few of the principal houses. At each Saint Nicholas calls in its due turn.

He enters with the two angels, leaving the demons outside to indulge in any pranks they will.

A great hush falls upon the assembled children as the Saint advances into the room. One by one he

No, I don't believe in you any more, but you may leave the things.

Drawing by J. R. Shaver.
Copyright 1908 by Life Publishing Co.

calls them up to examine them. Simple questions suited to their various ages are put to them by the bishop, after which each has to repeat a hymn or a prayer. All this part of the evening's business is carried on with the greatest seriousness and decorum on the part of children and grown-ups alike.

If the child passes a satisfactory examination the angels present it with nuts and apples—if not it has to stand aside. When the last of the examinations is over, the devils are admitted into the room.

They are not allowed to come near the good children, but they may tease and frighten the naughty little boys and girls as much as they choose. They delight in strange dances, and in all sorts of odd antics, such as smearing the girls' faces with lamp-black, or putting coal dust and ashes down the backs of the boys.

When Saint Nicholas has left, the children return to their own homes. Before going to bed they hang up their stockings by the chimney or, more likely, place their little boots and shoes close to the hearth, expecting to find them filled with gifts in the morning.

Boots and shoes indeed, came before stockings almost everywhere, the advantages of clean stockings as receivers for candies and other eatables being a comparatively new discovery. In Belgium to this day the children give their shoes an extra fine polish on Christmas Eve, fill them with hay, oats, carrots, for Santa Klaus's white horse, and put them on the table, or set them in the fireplace. The room is then carefully closed and the door is locked.

In the morning a strange thing is found to have happened! The furniture is all turned topsy-turvy, the fodder has been removed from the shoes and in its place the good little children find all sorts of nice things and the bad ones only rods of birch and bits of coal.

Boots and shoes are also in use in many parts of France. But here, as a general rule, it is the good little Jesus (le bon petit Jesus) who comes down the chimney to fill all this footgear with sweetmeats. Formerly this custom extended to Paris. A French journalist named Charton thus describes the sights that met his eye on Christmas eve in Paris in the middle of the nineteenth century:

"Lo! what a strange thing! Before all the mantelpieces of Paris are ranged, with a wonderful symmetry, charming little shoes, pretty little *bottines,* miniature slippers, and, as the extremities of the *faubourgs,* poor little sabots! It will be asked, what all those tiny little boots and shoes are doing there? There are enough of them to cover the feet of all the inhabitants of the vast kingdom of Lilliput. What are they doing there? They are waiting for a beau-

Santa Claus: "Whew! I suppose if I don't remember those poor boys in Wall Street they'll complain to Teddy."

Drawing by C. J. Taylor.

tiful little luminous hand to descend from heaven to fill them with preserved fruits and bonbons! In the olden time the presents intended for children were fastened to the two ends of the Yule Log. Later an attempt was made to introduce into France the Christmas-tree, which, in a large portion of Europe, has superseded the Yule Log. But it is most usual to keep to the simple custom of filling the little shoes with bonbons, which more than one mother of the laboring classes has had the foresight to reserve for that purpose. We will not venture to say that, whilst the good mother or the elder sister is stealthily approaching the hearth and stooping down, one of the little sleepers, kept awake with expectation, does not open his eyelids slily, and say to himself: 'Ah! I was sure it was not the little Jesus!' But the prudent child will take care not to confess that he has discovered the mystery; he has too much interest in being cheated next Christmas-day; and in a few hours the room will ring with his cries of false surprise but real gratification."

Only candies and sweetmeats, you will see, were brought down through the chimney by the Christ-child on Christmas eve. The favorite time for gift-making from parent to child, from child to parent, from friend to friend, was on New Year's Day. Hence that holiday is known as "Le Jour des Etrennes (the day of presents), "étrennes" being a corruption of the Latin word "strenae," the gifts exchanged during the Saturnalia, about which I have written in the fourth chapter of this book.

Though Saint Nicholas is honored as the patron of children in nearly all the Catholic countries of continental Europe, he is rarely associated in any way with Christmas. That day is there held sacred to the Christ child alone. In a very few localities Saint Nicholas may appear on his own day to find out what good little boys and girls would like to have on Christmas, or, sometimes, at New Year's, but it is generally the little Jesus who is the actual gift bringer.

In the Catholic portions of Austria and Germany all of the windows are lit up on the night of December 24 so as to enable Him to pick His way from house to house. Here you may again recognize a lingering memory of the Pagan and Jewish festivals wherein lighted torches, or lamps, or candles form a chief feature.

And, indeed, one may point out right here that the Christ child supplies another link with the old pagan Silenus. The latter, as I have told you, was, among other things, the guardian and tutor of the infant Bacchus. Whenever picture or statue represented him in this capacity all his evil traits were dropped. He became a very different being from the grace-

Santa Claus up in a balloon.
Copyright 1908 by Life Publishing Co.

less reveller of the Bacchanalian feasts.   He was now painted or carved as an old man, grave and sober, clean-cut in limbs and features, holding little Bacchus in his arms or on his shoulders.   Possibly this figure may have suggested the mediaeval legend of Saint Christopher, who, it is fabled, bore the Christ child on his shoulders across a river in Germany.

In Italy almost every church has an altar dedicated to the Christ child and decorated with a wooden or waxen effigy known as "Il Bambino," or "the babe."   On Christmas day this Bambino is specially honored by being dressed up in his finest clothes and placed in a mimic cradle, called a presepio.   All good Catholics flock to do the image honor during the twelve days from Christmas to Epiphany.

The most famous Bambino in Italy is that in the Franciscan church of Ara Cœli at Rome, which is believed to heal the sick and perform other miracles. On Christmas day a curious ceremony is performed in his honor which makes our thoughts travel back to the Boy-bishop of old England and elsewhere.   Opposite the presepio in which the little waxen figure reposes is built a palco, or platform, and on this platform a number of baby orators follow one another with little speeches, written by their elders, that dwell upon the birth of our Lord and the incidents of His childhood.

CHAPTER XVII

SAINT NICHOLAS IN AMERICA.

Just as the Christmas tree was brought over to this country by early German immigrants so Saint Nicholas, or Santa Klaus, came here in the train of the Dutch settlers of New York. He established himself first in the little island of Manhattan and then gradually spread all over the country, being greatly assisted by the fact that he was no stranger to the German settlers everywhere. But his Dutch origin is shown by the very name Santa Klaus, which is common alike to Holland and America, though it is elsewhere unknown.

At first he was honored on his own day with the same observances that marked the festival in the Fatherland.

Before the beginning of the nineteenth century, however, St. Nicholas's day had been all but forgotten in New Amsterdam (the Dutch name for New York) and we find that New Year's eve was the occasion when he made his rounds as a gift bearer to the children. Later he transferred his activities to Christmas.

New Year's gifts in a French workingman's family.

Drawing by Gavarni.

I reproduce from an old New York magazine,
dated January, 1844, a print which shows Santa
Klaus on the point of remounting a chimney after
filling the stockings of the children of the household.
The text expressly says that the time is New Year's
eve.

To go further back, we know that even in the
eighteenth century, when New York was still to a
great extent Dutch in blood and in feeling, the little
children of the Knickerbockers would gather expect-
ant around the great hearth in the parlor on the eve
of New Year and not on the eve of Saint Nicholas's
feast. It was to Saint Nicholas, however, that they
addressed the childish hymns and songs which their
forefathers had brought over from Holland.

Here are two specimen verses:

> Santa Klaus, good holy man!
> Go your way from Amsterdam;
> From Amsterdam to Spain,
> From Spain to Orange,
> And bring us little children toys.

> Saint Nicholas, my dear good friend,
> To praise you ever is my end.
> If you will presents to me give
> I'll serve you till I cease to live.

It was about the middle of the nineteenth century
that the funny men of America took the Saint under

their special patronage. In Holland he had been austere and dignified, as became a bishop and a saint. In America he developed into the fat, jolly, pot-bellied old roysterer whom we all know and love and who reminds us at so many points of the fun loving Silenus of Pagan times.

Undoubtedly it was the American Clement C. Moore who immortalized the figure and decided the model which all succeeding poets and artists have ever followed. This is how Santa Klaus is described in Mr. Moore's very popular poem entitled "A Visit from Santa Klaus":

> He was dressed all in fur from his head to his foot,
> And his clothes were all tarnished with ashes and soot;
> A bundle of toys he had flung on his back,
> And he looked like a pedlar just opening his pack,
> His eyes how they twinkled! his dimples how merry!
> His cheeks were like roses, his nose like a cherry.
> His droll little mouth was drawn up like a bow,
> And the beard on his chin was as white as the snow.
> The stump of a pipe he held tight in his teeth,
> And the smoke it encircled his head like a wreath,
> He had a broad face and a little round belly
> That shook, when he laughed, like a bowlful of jelly,
> He was chubby and plump — a right jolly old elf —
> And I laughed when I saw him, in spite of myself.

Year by year the funny men of the pencil and the pen do their best to add to his eccentricities yet always

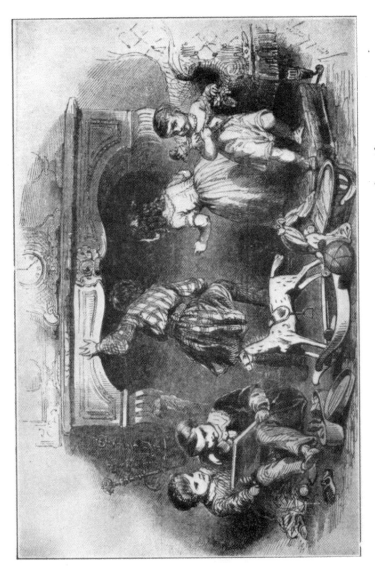

French children gazing up the chimney for gifts.

Old French print.

they retain a measure of respect for the dear old gentleman.

One comic artist sends him to Wall Street among the brokers and the bankers, yet he preserves his dignity even among those shrewd and clever men, and is ready to teach them more than they can hope to teach him.

Other artists make him turn to account the latest inventions of our inventors and scientists. Even if one picture does show him coming to grief on an automobile, another catches him in the very act of utilizing a flying machine.

Again we are shown another side of the matter. We are brought face to face with the unbelief of the child who is ripening into boyhood or girlhood.

At six years old or sometimes later doubts begin to visit the youthful mind. These doubts are carried very far by the little girl—a juvenile Saint Thomas in pantalettes—who in Mr. J. R. Shaver's picture, meets Santa Klaus face to face, yet tells him to his face that she doesn't believe in him.

At this period in their lives young folks of both sexes will sympathize with the spirit of inquiry that summons Saint Nicholas, as in Mr. O'Malley's cartoon, to answer before a judge and jury of their own age the question as to whether he has any real existence.

And now turn to the last picture of all, that which

Mr. Henry Hutt has kindly lent me for reproduction in this little book, and if you insist on an answer which will rob you of the bliss of ignorance, perhaps you will find it there!

THE END

Silenus and Bacchus.

Roman statue of the fourth century.

The bambino.

In the church of Ara Cocli, Rome.

Santa Klaus on New Year's eve.

From an early American print.

The investigating committee — Santa Claus to the Bar. Is he a
real person?

By Power O'Malley.
Copyright 1908 by Life Publishing Co.

St. Nicholas unveils.
By Henry Hutt.
Courtesy of the artist.